Measurement and Evaluation in Psychology and Education

Published by
Saurabh Publishing House

Measurement and Evaluation in Psychology and Education

K P Duggal

Saurabh
Publishing House
4735/22, Prakash Deep Building,
Ansari Road, Daryaganj
New Delhi- 110002

Published by
SAURABH PUBLISHING HOUSE

Distributed by:
Lotus Press Publishers & Distributors
Unit No. 220, Second Floor, 4735/22, Prakash Deep Building,
Ansari Road, Darya Ganj, New Delhi-110002
Ph: 23280047, 32903912, 098118-38000
www.lotuspress.co.in

Saurabh Publishing is an imprint of
Lotus Press Publishers & Distributors

Measurement and Evaluation in Psychology and Education

ISBN 978-81-89005-04-7 (PB)

Printed at : Concept Imprint.

PREFACE

Evaluation is an integral part of education. It affects the way students study, their motivation, performance and their aspirations. Its' ultimate aim is to improve student learning. It provides students, parents and teachers with valid information concerning student progress. It facilitates administrators, policy-makers and the society to have an idea of what is missing and what is available in our education system.

Evaluation involves determination of the types of data which needs to be collected, determination of the individual, group or groups from which data will be obtained, collection of data, analysis of data, interpretation of the data and decision-making. The use of educational assessments and the analysis of data such as scores obtained from assessments to infer the abilities and proficiencies of students is known as educational measurement.

Measurement and evaluation plays a significant role in effective planning of classroom instruction and determining the level of attainment of instructional objectives by students. It helps in the diagnosis of deficiency in learning, prognosis for determining the readiness for learning a specific task and placement of children in different groups and grades of the same school and different schools. The evaluation results are also helpful in determining the effectiveness of a course, programme and functioning of a school.

Designed for undergraduate or graduate level courses in psychological and educational measurement, the present book focuses on the basic aspects of measurement and evaluation in psychology and education. Incorporating standard measurement concepts as they apply to both educational and psychological assessments, it provides a technically rigorous treatment of the core issues in measurement in an easy-to-understand style. The book will enable the readers to understand the processes of evaluation, measurement and testing in a better a manner, and you will recognize the interconnections among curriculum, goals, objectives, testing and evaluation.

Author

CONTENTS

1

Fundamentals of Evaluation and Measurement

Evaluation is an integral component of all systems of education at all processes. It is what enables educators, teachers, administrators, policy-makers and the community have an idea of what is missing and what is available. Evaluation can be defined in two ways, depending on what we want to achieve at end of the exercise.

(a) Evaluation is the systematic process of collecting and analyzing data in order to determine whether, and to what degree objectives have or are being achieved.

(b) Evaluation is the systematic process of collecting and analyzing data in order to make decisions.

The first part of these definitions (systematic process of collecting and analyzing data) is common to both of the definitions provided here. However, the basic difference between the two definitions is the issue of whether decisions or judgements are an integral component of evaluation. The second definition seems to be more inclusive, as it does not preclude the activities implied in the first definition.

In most cases, evaluation is intended to answer questions that require some degree of valuing. Questions, such as

(a) Is the special programme worth what it costs?

(b) Is the new experimental reading curriculum better than the previous one?

(c) Should Mr. Shetty be placed in a programme for the gifted?

require the collection and analysis of data and interpretation of that data with respect to one or more criteria. The more objective the criteria, the better, although some degree of subjectivity is unavoidable since people are making the final judgement. In finding answers to the above questions, evaluation is not merely concerned with determining whether something is 'good' or 'bad'. The function or purpose of evaluation is to determine the current status of the object of evaluation compare the status with a set of standards or criteria select an alternative in order to make decision.

At the end of the process, there may be only two alternatives or a combination of complex activities and programs designed as intervention for the current situation. In general, the process of evaluation involves determination of the types of data which needs to be collected, determination of the individual, group or groups from which data will be obtained, collection of data, analysis of data, interpretation of the data and decision-making.

Decision based on valid procedures is critical because although all decisions are not equally important, each one has a consequence which directly or indirectly affects students. The more serious the consequence, the more important the decision. Every educational decision, however, should be made on rational, objective basis to the greatest degree possible and should be based on the best data available.

The data collected during the evaluation process are only as good as the measurements upon which the measurements are based. Measurement is the process of quantifying the degree to which someone or something possesses a give trait, i.e. quality, characteristic or feature.

Measurements permits more objective description concerning traits and facilitates comparisons. Thus, instead of saying that Shyama is underweight for her age and height, we can say that Shyama is 16 years old, 5'8' tall, and weighs only 48 Kg. Further, instead of saying Shyama is more intelligent than Rima, we can say Shyama has a measured IQ of 125 and Rima has a measured IQ of 88. In each case, the numerical statement is more precise, more objective, and less open to interpretation than the corresponding verbal description.

There is more professional disagreement about whether all traits of interest can be measured. Can you really measure elusive qualities such as empathy, appreciation, motivation or interests? Can you really measure values and attitudes? The answer is yes, but it is not easy. Supporters of this position put forth the following argument: if something exists, it exists in quantities; if it exists in quantities, it can be measured. If you accept this logic, any trait of interest to educators can be measured. Thus, the purpose of educational measurement is to represent how much of 'something' is possessed by a person or entity.

Agreeing that at least theoretically all things can be measured and measuring them are two quite different processes. Valid measurements in education is not easy. The major problem is that, with the exception of measurement of physical characteristics such as height and weight, all measurement is indirect; there are no yardsticks or scales for measuring traits like intelligence, achievement or attitude. Assessment of such traits must be of necessity be based upon inference. The problem is further complicated by the lack of well-validated instruments. In some areas, the problem is not as serious as in others.

The term measurement is not synonymous with the administration of pen-and-pencil tests. Data may be collected via processes such as observation and analysis and rating of a product. In some cases, required data may already be available and retrievable from records. In many cases, however, some combination of standardized and/or self-developed tests is required.

TYPES OF EVALUATION

When we speak of the types of evaluation, we are referring to the different processes, products and persons subject to evaluation. These include student, curricula, schools, school systems, large populations, special programs or projects and personnel. The fact that we speak of different types of evaluation does not mean that there are a number of different evaluation processes. The basic evaluation process is the same, regardless of what is being evaluated. What differs is what is being evaluated, how the evaluation process is applied and the types of decisions made. Depending upon what is being evaluated, different types of data will be collected, different criteria will be applied to the data, and different types of decisions will be made. But the basic evaluation process is the same and the same general concepts and principles of measurement and evaluation are applicable.

Student Evaluation

Achievement is one of the variables on which student is assessed; other major variables include aptitude, intelligence, personality, attitudes and interests. In order to assess achievement, tests, both standardized and teacher-made, are administered; projects, procedures and oral presentations are rated; and formal and informal observations are made. A teacher uses performance data not only to evaluate student progress but also to evaluate his/her own instruction. In other words, the process of evaluating students provides feedback to the teacher. Feedback on current student progress also gives direction to future instructional activities.

There are all kinds of decisions made which do directly affect the student; not all of these decisions are made by the teacher. The teacher decides:

- Whether the student has achieved objectives, or to what degree, and provides appropriate remedial work if necessary
- Whether the student is working up to a potential
- What should be expected from a certain student or a group of students
- Whether the child has special needs which cannot be met in regular classroom and recommend that a child be placed in special environment

There are numerous other decisions that are made concerning students in which the teacher is either not involved or only makes recommendations. These decisions include

- The placement of a child in a special programme
- Promotion of a student
- The employment of students and their admission to other educational institutions

Curriculum Evaluation

Curriculum evaluation involves the evaluation of any instructional programme or instructional materials, and includes evaluation of such factors as instructional strategies, textbooks, audiovisual materials, and physical and organizational arrangements. Curriculum evaluation may involve evaluation of a total package or evaluation of one small aspect of a total curriculum, such as a film. Although ongoing programmes are subject to evaluation, curriculum evaluation is usually associated with innovation, a new or different approach; the approach may be general or specific to a given area.

Curriculum evaluation usually involves both internal and external criteria and comparisons. Internal evaluation is concerned with whether the new process or product achieves its stated objectives, that is whether it does what it purports to do, as well as with evaluation of the objectives themselves. External evaluation is concerned with whether the process or the product does whatever it does better than some other process or product.

In addition to student achievement, there are a number of other factors which should be considered during curriculum evaluation. The two most important factors are attitude and cost. Research has demonstrated that there is a proportional relationship between teacher attitude toward curriculum and its ultimate effectiveness.

Curriculum evaluation has one major problem associated with it: It is very difficult to compare fairly the effectiveness of one programme or approach with another. Even if two programmes deal with the same subject area, they may deal with objectives which are very different, and it is very difficult to find a test or other measures which is equally fair, or valid for both programmes. If one curriculum is to compared to another, the objectives of each must be examined carefully; if no measure can be located which is equally appropriate to both, then one must be developed that is.

School Evaluation

Evaluation of a school involves evaluation of the total educational programme of the school and entails the collection of data on all aspects of its functioning. The purpose of the school evaluation is to determine the degree to which school objectives are being met and to identify areas of strength and weakness in the total programme. Information from school programme provides feedback to which gives direction to the future activities of the school and results in decision concerning the allocation of school resources.

One major component of school evaluation is the school testing programme; the more comprehensive the testing program, the more valuable are the resulting data. A school testing programme should include measurement of achievement, aptitude, personality and interest. Test selected for a school must match the objectives of the school and be appropriate for the students to be tested.

In general, school evaluation involves more than the administration of tests to students; it may require any combination of questionnaires, interviews, and observations with data being collected from all persons in the school community, including administration, teachers and counsellors.

Evaluation of Large Populations

Evaluation of large populations involves assessing the current status and the educational progress of large number of students, typically distributed over a large geographic region. State-wide assessment programmes are generally based on the premises that the state system of education is responsible for student achievement of certain basic skills required for effective functioning in our society, and that programmes designed to promote achievement of the basic skills should be as effective and economical as possible. One of the major aims of state assessment is to provide information to state and local decision makers about the adequacy of basic educational programme. State-wide assessment typically involves measurement of minimum educational objectives and selected optional objectives using both criterion-references and norm-referenced

Evaluation of Special Projects and Programmes

Special projects and programmes include all those organized efforts which are not, strictly speaking, part of the regular school programme; they are typically innovative in nature and the duration of their existence is dependent upon their success. Whether it is required or not, conduction of evaluation is in the best interest of a project or programme since it is the only valid way to very its effectiveness.

Evaluation of Personnel

Evaluation of personnel (staff evaluation) includes evaluation of all persons responsible, either directly or indirectly, for educational outcomes, i.e., teachers, administrators, counsellors and so forth. It has been found out that this area of evaluation is very complicated; it is difficult to determine what behaviours are to be evaluated. The best solution to problem of personnel evaluation is to collect the best and most data possible, from as many sources as possible.

PHASES OF EVALUATION

Evaluation is a continuous process; contrary to public opinion, it is not what you do at the end. Evaluation should be planned for prior to execution of any effort and should be involved throughout the duration of the activity. There are typically a series of temporary ends in a continuous cycle. In student evaluation, for example, we start with a set of instructional objectives. Ten we implement instructional strategies to facilitate their achievement. Ten we measure achievement, a temporary end in the instructional cycle. Based on the results, we reassess our objectives and strategies and proceed. Thus the process is cyclic, with feedback from one cycle guiding the next. We do not just evaluate outcomes; every stage of the process is subject to evaluation beginning with the objectives.

The evaluation process entails decision-making. Any educational endeavour involves a whole host of decisions which must be made—decisions about objectives, decisions about strategies, decisions about measurement, and so forth. These various decisions can be classified in terms of when they are made, that is, during what stage of the activity under study. Thus, each phase of evaluation involves different kind of decisions. Logically we can identify three phases; the planning phase, the process phase and the product phase.

The Planning Phase

This initial phase of evaluation takes place prior to actual implementation and involves making decisions about what course of action will be taken and toward what ends. The planning phase involves a number of processes which are discusses below.

(a) Situation analysis

The first step is to analyze the situation as it presently exists in order to establish the parameters of the effort. This step includes activities such as the collection of background information and assessment of existing constraints. For a teacher this may involve examination of the commutative records of his or her students in order to get a frame of reference based on their abilities and histories. After the parameters have been established, more realistic goals and objectives can be formulated.

(b) Specification of objectives

Goals are general statements of purpose, or desired outcomes and not as such directly measurable. Each goal must be translated into one or more specific objectives which are measurable. Thus, objectives are specific statements of what is to be accomplished and how well and are expressed in terms of quantifable, measurable outcomes. Objectives may process oriented or product oriented. Process objectives describe outcomes desired during the execution of the effort, and they related to the development and execution. Product objectives, on the other hand, describe outcomes intended as a result of the effort.

Objectives give direction to all subsequent activities and achievement of objectives is ultimately measured. Objectives, whether instructional or program objectives, form the foundation of all subsequent evaluation activities, and therefore it is critical that they themselves be evaluated in terms of both relevance, measurability, substance, and technical accuracy.

(c) Specification of pre-requisites

Objectives entail unique procedure with respect to student evaluation. In most cases, specification of a given set of instructional objectives is based on the assumption that students have already acquired certain skills and knowledge. If the assumption is incorrect, then the objectives are not appropriate. The assumed behaviours are referred to as pre-requisites or entry behaviours. Systematic instruction and evaluation require that these pre-requisites be specified and measured. Assessment of entry behaviour is specifically important at the beginning of any instructional unit. To arrive at pre-requisites, you simply ask yourself the following question: What must any students know or be able to do prior to instruction order to benefit from instruction and achieve any objectives.

(d) Selection and development of measuring instruments

Collection of data to determine degree of achievement of objectives requires administration of one or more instruments. Such instruments must either be developed or selected. Selection of an instrument involves examining those that are available and selecting the best one. Best, in this case, means the one that is most appropriate for your objectives and users. Development of a good instrument takes considerable time, effort and skill. Training in measurement in the process is necessary for such end.

(e) Delineation of strategies

Strategies are generally approaches to promoting achievement of one or more objectives. There may be instructional strategies, curriculum strategies, and program strategies. Each strategy entails a number of specific activities, and there are typically a number of strategies to choose from. Execution of these strategies must be planned for, to ensure the availability of necessary resources. Strategies which must be thoroughly thought of before evaluation is conducted include: task analysis, review of concepts, sequencing, provision of feedback and practice.

(f) Preparation of time schedule

Preparation of realistic time schedule is important for all types of evaluation; rarely do we have as long as we please to conduct evaluation. Basically a time schedule includes a list of the major activities of the proposes evaluation effort and corresponding expected initiation and completion times for each activity. You should allow yourself enough time, so that if an unforeseen minor delay occurs, you can still meet your final deadline.

The Process Phase

The process phase involves making decisions based upon events which occur during actual implementation of the planned instruction, programme or project. The first step in the process phase is to administer pre-tests, if such are appropriate. Based on the pre-test results, decisions may be made concerning the appropriateness of the already specified objectives. Following initial testing, planned strategies and activities are executed in the predetermined sequence. Data collected during this phase provide feedback concerning whether execution is taking place as planned and whether and whether strategies and activities are being effective. The basic purposes of this phase are to determine whether the effort is being executed as intended, to determine the degree of achievement of process objectives, and to identify ways in which improvements can be made. The process phase is referred to as formative evaluation.

The Product Phase

The product phase involves making decisions at the end or more likely at the end of one cycle of instruction, a programme or a project. Decisions made during the product phase are based on the results of the post-tests an on other cumulative types of data. The major purpose of the product phase is to collect data in order to make decisions concerning the overall effectiveness of instruction, a programme or project. During this phase it is determined whether and/or what degree intended product objectives were achieved. Data analysis and interpretation is followed by the preparation of a report which describes the objectives, procedures, and outcomes of the effort. The results of the product phase of evaluation are used in at least in two major ways:

(a) They provide feedback and direction to all who are were involved in the effort.

(b) They provide feedback to outside decision makers, such as parents, principals, school board members and funding sources.

Results of the product phase need to be interpreted with care. Failure to meet objectives, for example, is not necessarily fatal; degree of achievement needs to be considered. The product phase of evaluation is referred to as summative evaluation.

SPECIFICATION OF OBJECTIVES

At the heart of all evaluation and assessment activities in education stands objectives, which give direction to the process of education. Objectives help us what to measure and how to measure. They indicate whether the process of education has been successful, and what can be done to may it so. In this activity, learners will be able learn what objectives are and their importance in education. In addition, learners will master the types and components of educational objectives.

Nature of Objectives

Objectives are specific statements of what is to be accomplished and how well, and are expressed in terms of quantifable, measurable outcomes. Objectives are executed prior to execution of an effort and are subject to technical and substantative review. An instructional objective is an intent communicated by a statement describing a proposed change in a learner—a statement of what the learner is to be like when he or she has successfully completed a learning experience. Learning is an inferred event, not directly observable one; thus it must be determined what behaviour, or performance, will constitute sufcient evidence that the desired ability exists. Whether a capability is acquired, or learned, as a result of instruction can only be determined by observing performance at two different points in time; before and after instruction, and seeing whether performance has changed. Learning per se cannot be directly observed or measured, changes in performance can be.

Objectives give direction or guide activities of an effort. The set general strategy and activities for their attainment. This means that different set of objectives will usually generate different strategies and thus activities. Some people argue that objectives produce rigid, conforming procedures, standards and behaviours which discourage creativity and spontaneity and fail to take into consideration individual differences. They also question whether all educational outcomes can be objectified. They support their argument that we tend to select objectives that are easier to measure, not necessary important. However, it should be noted that most of the desired outcomes can be expressed in observable, measurable terms.

Needs Assessment

It would be virtually impossible for the educational system to attempt to foster achievement of all possible objectives; formally or informally, each educational endeavour must select and put in priority order the goals and objectives with which it will be concerned. Conceptually if there is a gap between the way things are (current status or status quo) and the way we would like them to be (desired outcome), there is a *need*. Depending upon how specifically a need has been defined, it can be translated into either a goal or an objective, the intent being to eliminate the need. Needs assessment is the process of identifying needs and establishing relative priority of those needs. The basic goals and objectives of the educational system have remained relatively stable but the emphasis or priorities have shifted over time. Needs assessment can be applied to, and used by all levels and components of the educational system, including classrooms, programmes, projects, schools, school systems, states and countries.

Types of Objectives

Objectives look basically look the same regardless of the type of evaluation, all objectives indicated intended outcomes. One basic difference is that certain types of evaluation, and their corresponding objectives, are primarily concerned with the performance of individuals, whereas others are primarily concerned with the performance of groups.

Literally, thousands and thousands of objectives, covering virtually every area of instruction, have been written to express desired student behaviours. In contrast, very little exists in terms of performance objectives for teachers, even less for administrators, and essentially nothing for special programme and project personnel; this is due mainly to the lack of empirical evidence linking given behaviours with job success.

(a) Competency-based objectives

The objectives or competencies to be achieved by students in various programmes are typically developed by university or college instructors, experts in their respective felds, and reviewed by appropriate public school or community groups. The intent of the competency-based objectives is to communicate behaviours believed to be required for successful job performance and to have students demonstrate these behaviours prior to graduation.

(b) Mastery objectives

Certain instructional objectives are considered to be required, minimum essentials, i.e., objectives which should be achieved by virtually all students, regardless of ability or background; these are referred to as mastery objectives, or minimum skills, objectives. In mastery system, the amount learned, as indicated in the objective, is constant; instruction is individualized and the amount time required to achieve these objectives varies from one student to another.

Taxonomy of Educational Objectives

The taxonomies classify all objectives into a hierarchy of categories based on presumed complexity. Each succeeding category involves behaviours believed to be more complex than the one previous and each considered be pre-requisite to the next. The stated purpose of the taxonomies is to facilitate communication. The existence of taxonomies also focuses attention on a wide range of behaviour outcomes, thus making it less likely that all the objectives for a given effort will involve lower level behaviours only. It is believed that all instructional objectives can be classified as belonging to one of the three taxonomies or domains—cognitive, affective and psychomotor.

1. The Cognitive Domain

The taxonomy of cognitive objectives has definitely made educators aware of the wide range of abilities involved in cognitive learning. Each of the six major categories represents a different kind of learning process. The major categories of the cognitive taxonomy of educational objectives are as follows:

(a) Knowledge

(b) Comprehension

(c) Application

(d) Analysis

(e) Synthesis

(f) Evaluation

Robert Gagne has approached classification of the types of learning from a different angle. He believes that types or classes of learning can be categorized based on the conditions of instruction necessary to facilitate learning of each type. Gagne has distinguished eight classes of learning and corresponding instructional conditions for learning that are associated with them:

(a) signal learning

(b) stimulus-response learning

(c) chaining

(d) verbal association

(e) discrimination learning

(f) concept learning, and

(g) problem solving

In the past, educators have been criticized for paying too much attention to cognitive outcomes and not being concerned enough with the feelings and attitudes of students. The affective domain deals with such outcomes.

2. *The Affective Domain*

The taxonomy of affective objectives deals with outcomes that are much more difficult to promote and to measure, intangibles such as feelings, attitudes, interests and values. The affective categories represents a hierarchy of acceptance which ranges from willingness to receive, or attend, to characterization by a value. Aswith all objectives, the intent is to identify observable, measurable behaviours from which we can infer learning; this is clearly more difficult for affective outcomes. Achievement of affective objectives can be determined through the administration of self-report measures which entail a number of problems.

The major categories of the affective taxonomy of educational objectives are as follows;

(*a*) Receiving

(*b*) Responding

(*c*) Valuing

(*d*) Organization

(*e*) Characterization by value

3. The Psychomotor Domain

The psychomotor domain entails physical abilities, those involving muscular or motor skills, manipulation of objectives, or neuromuscular coordination. The task for taxonomy development in the psychomotor domain is more complex than for other domains. Tough there isn't widely accepted categories for this domain, the following is used in some of the literature on the area.

(*a*) Refex

(*b*) Fundamental movements

(*c*) Perceptual abilities

(*d*) Physical abilities

(*e*) Skilled movements

(*f*) Non-discursive communication

Levels of Specificity

Objectives can be written at varying levels of specificity. At one end of the continuum we have very broad statements of long-term outcomes; these are generally referred to as goals or general objectives. At the other end of the spectrum we have very precise statements of more immediate outcomes, each representing one behaviour or outcome; these are generally referred to as specific objectives.

Goals/General Objectives

Goals are global statements of long-term outcomes. The achievement of such goals or generally objectives cannot be directly measured directly. Goals of education tend to be established at the national level.

Intermediate Objectives

Goals are frequently translated into intermediate objectives. Objectives at this level are more precise than general objectives but not as detailed as specific objectives. They are in various situations referred to as cumulative objectives, course objectives and tasks. Such objectives are usually measureable and typically represent more complex behaviours expected as a result of achievement of a number of pre-requisite specific objectives.

Specific Objectives

Specifc objectives deal with the most discrete intended outcomes. They are measurable outcomes upon which day-to-day activities such as instruction are based. The task analysis procedure is a method of translating cumulative objectives into specific objectives.

An objective can be so vague that it is ambiguous or so detailed that it is trivial and impractical. A sensible guiding principle suggests that each objective should represent a distinct task. A task can be defined as the smallest component of performance which has a distinct and independent purpose. The more simply worded objective is clearly more functional.

Stating Objectives

Selection or development of an objective is really the most important part of any educational programme. The objective gives direction to all other components of the programme, including the content, methodology to be used for instruction and assessment. First and foremost, we need to evaluate the specificity of the objective. An objective should communicate the intended outcome well enough that any evaluator will assess it in essentially the same way and be able to tell whether it had been achieved.

Components of Objectives

(a) Behaviour

The behaviour component of an objective indicates what will happen, or as in the case of instructional objectives, what observable measurable performance will constitute satisfactory evidence that the desired learning has occurred. An objective should state the intended learning outcome using an action verb that represents an observable outcome. Each objectives should entail an achievement of only one and behaviour, otherwise measurement of achievement becomes confounded.

(b) Condition

The conditions of an objective are the 'givens,' the context within which the behaviour will be exhibited. Conditions usually specify necessary materials, allowable resources, or imposed restrictions, and the word 'given' is not necessarily used.

(c) Criterion

When stated, the criterion component of an objective is the part that tells us how well the behaviour must be performed. It is the standard against which actual performance is compared. If the criterion is obvious or 100 per cent, it is not generally stated.

EVALUATION IN EDUCATIONAL PROCESS

The main purpose of classroom teaching is to influence student behaviour in the desired direction. The desired direction is guided by the educational objectives formulated by the school and the teacher. The teacher first of all, must be conscious of the goals and aims of education. More specifically, the teacher must formulate instructional objectives for various lessons and units in the systematized and rearranged syllabus in a subject of study. Secondly, the teacher should be in a position to construct effective learning experiences on the basis of student learning and the modes of effective communication channels. Finally, the teacher will determine the extent to which these objectives are being achieved. Hence, three major elements in the education process are objectives, learning experiences and learner appraisal. The simple representation of educational process is shown below:

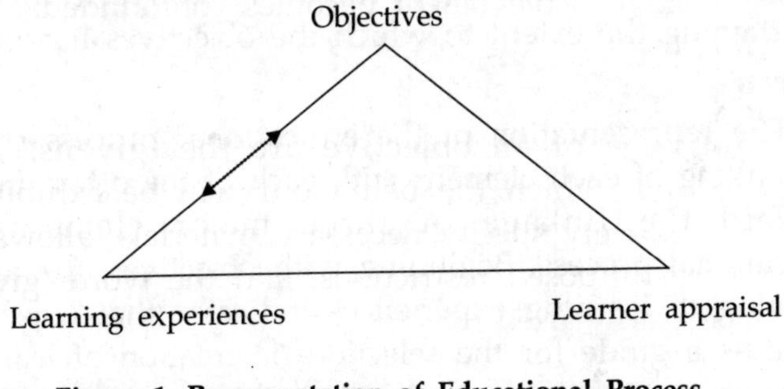

Figure 1. Representation of Educational Process

The above representation is a dynamic one and shows interaction among three major elements as shown by directional arrows. Objectives refer to one's intention of desired behaviour that learners should acquire. The term learning experiences, refers to those activities and experiences that the learners undergo in order to acquire the desired behaviours.

The teacher plays an important role in providing learning experiences. Learning experiences involve interaction of students and content with the help of a teacher. The teacher uses various teaching methods and techniques for providing learning experiences to the learner. These learning experiences lead to behavioural changes among learners. So, learning involves modification in the behaviour of a learner through learning experiences. In order that there may be an appreciable learning on the part of students, it is important that teaching must be effective. The teacher must provide situations for close interaction of students with content by using appropriate teaching methods and techniques. Hence effective teaching leads to successful learning experiences.

Besides teaching, the learning experiences can also be brought about through a number of ways such as the library, laboratory readings, radio, films, film strips, science clubs, field trips or such other learning situations in real life. Learner appraisal is concerned with ascertaining the extent to which the objectives have been met.

The representation of the educational process shows the linking of each element with each of the other. Let us explain the linkage of three major elements of educational process. Beginning with objectives, the arrow pointing to learning experiences indicates that objectives serve as a guide for the selection or creation of learning experiences. For example, if a geometry course is aimed at developing deductive thinking abilities in learners, then learning experiences require work other than geometry content. This may include home assignment to work on newspaper editorials, advertisements and also individual projects. The point is that the nature of one's objectives will be an important determinant of the learning experiences that constitute the operational programme. The arrow pointing from objectives to learner appraisal indicates that the primary focus of appraisal is on gathering evidence on the extent to which the objectives of the programme have been attained. Just as objectives provide specification for establishment of learning experiences, they also furnish specifications for learner appraisal. For example, the development of deductive thinking among students, might require in its appraisal of learning, the evidence regarding students' proficiency to apply deductive principles to the analysis of a variety of material in life situations, which may be outside the field of geometry.

Now, the arrow pointing from learning experiences to learner appraisal is indicative of the fact that learning experiences, provide examples for the development of appraisal tasks. The objectives that the students are engaged in, during the learning phase of the programme, should furnish ideas for appraisal situations. Thus, the arrow pointing from learning experiences to learner appraisal, indicates that learning experiences furnish ideas and suggestions for learner appraisal. The appraisal task may not be identical but contain an element of novelty for the learner.

The two arrows pointing from learner appraisal to objectives and to learning experiences are especially important. In the case of the former, the arrow signifies that appraisal procedures should furnish information about the extent to which the objectives are being attained. In addition, appraisal information can furnish valuable information that may result in the modification of some objectives and the elimination of others. The appraisal helps in providing a solution to the following questions:

- Should the objectives be modified or perhaps eliminated?
- Are the objectives realistic for the particular group of learners?
- Are the necessary references available for achieving the objectives?

The arrow-pointing from learner appraisal to learning experiences, is suggestive of two important notions. First, it provides information about the extent to which learning experiences appear to be working well. Hence appraisal procedure can suggest the modification or elimination of learning experiences. A second important idea suggested by the arrow pointing from appraisal to learning experiences is that tasks, experiences and problems developed by evaluation specialist may be suggestive of new learning experiences. The incorporation of moral and imaginative appraisal materials into the learning phase of a programme has contributed significantly to the improvement of learning experiences.

The last arrow, which points from learning experiences to objectives, denotes that learning activities can result in encounters involving teachers, learners and learning materials which in turn may suggest new objectives.

Role of Evaluation

Evaluation plays an enormous role in the teaching-learning process. In learning, it contributes to formulation of objectives, designing of learning experiences and assessment of learner performance. Besides this, it is very useful to bring improvement in teaching and curriculum. It provides accountability to the society, parents, and to the education system. Let us discuss its uses briefly.

(a) *Teaching*: Evaluation is concerned with assessing the effectiveness of teaching, teaching strategies, methods and techniques. It provides feedback to the teachers about their teaching and the learners about their learning.

(b) *Curriculum*: The improvement in courses/curricula, texts and teaching materials is brought about with the help of evaluation.

(c) *Society*: Evaluation provides accountability to society in terms of the demands and requirements of the employment market.

(d) *Parents*: Evaluation mainly manifests itself in a perceived need for regular reporting to parents.

In brief, evaluation is a very important requirement for the education system. It fulfils various purposes in systems of education like quality control in education, selection/entrance to a higher grade or tertiary level. It also helps one to take decisions about success in specific future activities arid provides guidance to further studies and occupation. Some of the educationists view evaluation virtually synonymous with what was previously defined as learner appraisal, but evaluation has an expanded role. It plays an effective role in questioning or challenging the objectives. This does not mean that one can loosely criticise programme objectives. One should question or challenge programme objectives only after careful study of the relationship between a programme's objectives and the need for which the programme was designed. Evaluation helps a lot in the design and modification of learning experiences on the basis of feedback received by learner appraisal.

IMPORTANCE OF EVALUATION

Evaluation is inevitable in teaching-learning process. It is as inevitable in classroom teaching as it is in all fields of activity when judgements need to be made, however simple or complex the consideration involved. All of us are well aware, that during the course of a school day, teachers, principals and other school personnel make many decisions about students and help them to make many decisions for themselves. Effective decision-making process involves evaluation. For example, the division of students into various categories, or ranks within the total group, involves measurement of their achievement and interpretation of these. The need of evaluation is so intrinsic to the teaching-learning situation that even hasty consideration seems to indicate the advantages of a systematic use of planned evaluation. Evaluation helps teachers to make better evaluative judgements. All of us are aware that we carry out activities in various aspects of teaching-learning process like:

(a) fulfil classroom objectives

(b) diagnose learning difficulties of students

(c) determine readiness for new learning experiences

(d) form students' classroom groups for special activities

(e) assist students in their problems of adjustment

(f) prepare reports of pupils' progress.

In all these activities, we cannot escape making evaluative judgements. Decisions must be made and action must be taken. The more accurately we judge our pupils, the more effective we will be in directing their learning. The understanding of the principles and procedures of evaluation is very much needed in making more intelligent decisions in directing pupils progress towards worthwise educational goals.

EVALUATION, ASSESSMENT AND MEASUREMENT

Evaluation, particularly educational evaluation, is a series of activities that are designed to measure the effectiveness of the teaching-learning system as a whole. We are already familiar with the fact that the teaching-learning process involves interaction of three major elements i.e., objectives, learning experiences and learner appraisal. Evaluation takes care of all the interactive aspects of three major elements i.e., the whole teaching-learning system. It can be put in the following simple form as suggested by Mary Thorpe.

> Evaluation is the collection, analysis and interpretation of information about any aspect of a programme of education, as part of a recognised process of judging its effectiveness, its efficiency and any other outcomes it may have.

The above definition offers the following:

(*a*) Evaluation is not just another, word for assessment. The quality of our learners' learning may well be one of the outcomes we need to evaluate. But many other factors may be equally worth looking at.

(*b*) 'Any other outcomes' reminds us that evaluation should be capable of picking up the unexpected e.g. unwanted side effects or interesting new possibilities.

(*c*) 'By recognized process', it means that evaluation needs to be systematic, planned and openly discussed. It is not just keeping records or writing a final report.

(*d*) It is a public commitment to purposeful enquiry. As we have already discussed, evaluation according to Beeby's definition is "the systematic collection and interpretation of evidence leading as a part of process to a judgement of value with a view to action.

Assessment

By assessment, we mean the processes and instruments that are designed to measure the learner's achievement, when learners are engaged in an instructional programme of one sort or another. It is concerned with ascertaining the extent to which the objectives of the programme have been met. The term assessment is often used interchangeably with the terms evaluation and measurement. However, assessment has a narrower meaning than evaluation but a broader meaning than measurement. In its derivation, the word assess means "to sit beside" or "to assist the judge". It, therefore, seems appropriate in evaluation studies to limit the term assessment to the process of gathering the data and fashioning them into an interpretable form; judgement can then be made on the basis of this assessment. Let us take an example of testing of school children by Secondary Board. Tests are administered in reading, writing, science and other academic areas. Based on the information provided by the Secondary Board, educators, citizens and political leaders then make judgements about the effectiveness of the education system. Assessment the, as we define it, precedes the final decision making stage in evaluation e.g., the decision to continue, modify, or terminate an educational programme.

Measurement

It is mainly concerned with collection or gathering of data e.g. students' scores in an examination. It is an act or process of measuring physical properties of objects such as length and mass. Similarly, in behavioural sciences, it is concerned with measurement of psychological characteristics such as neuroticism, and attitudes towards various phenomena. The measurement involves assigning a score on a given task performed by the learner e.g., 33/50 i.e., thirty three out of fifty.

Thus, we find that evaluation involves assessment and measurement. It is a wider and more inclusive term than assessment and measurement. It can be represented as:

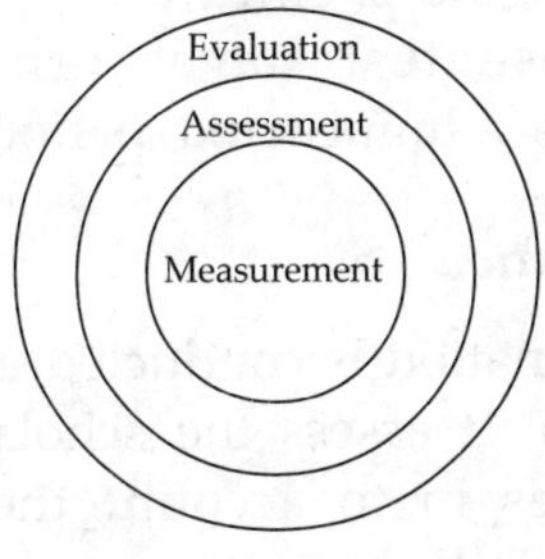

Hence evaluation process is quite comprehensive and it is very much desired for effective teaching and learning.

Let us explain the need and use of some of terms commonly used in the context of evaluation in our schools.

Examination

This term is used in schools to find out the growth of students in terms of their scholastic achievement. The examinations are conducted at different stages throughout the year. Let us briefly discuss them.

Semester, Half-yearly, Annual Examinations: In semester system, the assessment of the child is done after completion of courses meant for one semester. The academic session consisting of two semesters. The course of first semester will not be assessed again in the second semester or later, while some portion of the course content which was assessed in the half-yearly examinations or periodic tests may be assessed again in an annual examination.

Periodic Tests

These are used to assess the scholastic achievement of children after providing instruction for a specified period. The period may be one or two months. Some schools also call these periodic tests, Monthly tests, Terminal tests. The purpose of these tests is two fold; (*a*) to provide feedback to children and teachers about the achievement of children, (*b*) to help children in; improving their weaknesses, These test have formative nature of evaluation and are administered periodically.

Half-yearly Examination

This type of examination is conducted after completion of half of the session. It assess the scholastic aspect of the child. It also takes in to account the achievement of children in the periodic test. Its purpose is also two-fold i.e. assessing the performance and improving upon the weakness of the child. Half-yearly examination does not mean end of a part of the syllabus, not to be tested again.

Annual Examination

It is conducted after completion of one full year or academic session. It assesses the growth of children in terms of scholastic aspects to be achieved in one session. The important purpose of annual exams are, (*i*) grading, (*ii*) certification, (*iii*) promotion into next class or standard besides the results in the annual examination, the weightage may also be provided to the achievement in periodic tests and half-yearly examinations.

It is worthwhile to know the commonly used tools/ techniques in our schools.

Test

It provides a situation or a series of situations to students to find out their performance in terms of scores. The scores are known as marks. The tool used to test the performance is in terms of a set of questions called, Question Paper. These tests are also called achievement tests as they concentrate mainly on the scholastic achievement of the child.

Assessment of Non-scholastic Aspects of Students

To assess the social or/and personal qualities of students like regularity, punctuality, discipline, the habit of cleanliness, interests and attitude etc., the teacher uses a rating scale. The rating may be done on a different number of points e.g., three points or five points, depending upon the requirement of the teacher. Criteria for rating every activity may be prepared in a three or five or any other point scale and separate proforma may be evolved for each activity. Marks obtained by each student on the basis of the criteria may be entered in the column provided for them. These marks may be added and the average calculated. At the end of each term the teacher awards grades in each activity related to the personal and social qualities of the student.

Evaluation is aimed at students' development. Feedback from evaluation must be made available to the students and help them to prove their current strengths and weaknesses. By knowing their strength and weakness, students can think of further improvement. Evaluation should suggest all the needful requirements for their improvement. The requirements may be in terms of improvement in the content to be taught, teaching methods and style of learning. Hence, evaluation is very useful in diagnosing weakness and remedying them.

2

Psychological Measurement

Psychological measurement is the development of procedures to measure people's characteristics like intelligence or personality. The aptitude for a job or the presence of emotional disturbance can be determined applying standardized tests. Also known as psychological assessment or testing, it can be employed for researching or for predicting a future behavior. To be of utility, a test must meet the conditions of being valid and reliable. Its results must also be compared to a reference group.

A test is valid when it measures what it is supposed to measure. In psychology, there are many qualities that would be interesting to measure, yet it is difficult for psychologists to arrive at a definition. Without a clear and precise definition of the property in question, a test free of ambiguity is difficult to design. Intelligence tests are a well-known example of this difficulty: as psychologists do not agree on the definition of intelligence, the controversies on intelligence test scores are permanent.

Reliability is the condition of giving consistent results over time. During a test's design, it is given to the same people with intervals, and the parts of the test that produce inconsistent results are corrected. To be reliable, a test must be free of subjective considerations. Adjustments may be needed to judging criteria to meet this requirement. To be meaningful, the result of an individual's test must be compared to an adequate reference group. Such group is usually defined by characteristics such as age, grade in school, or occupation. The results of a comparison group are called 'norms.' Very often the raw result of a test for a person is modified so that it gives immediately the relation with the reference group. Those scores are said to be 'standardized.'

Apart from testing, other activities related with psychological measurement are observation and interviewing. Observation is used primarily with children, but it can also be applied to adults, either alone or in groups. For example, interaction among children can be observed at a playground, or the conduct of a mother and his child can be observed through a one-way mirror. Interviews, although very widely used, do not have the properties of reliability and validity unless they are carried out with these goals in mind, which is not usual. They should, therefore, be used only for orienting purposes.

PSYCHOMETRICS

The field of study concerned with the theory and technique of psychological measurement is known as psychometrics. It includes the measurement of knowledge, abilities, attitudes, personality traits, and educational measurement. The field is primarily concerned with the construction and validation of measurement instruments such as questionnaires, tests, and personality assessments. It involves two major research tasks, namely:

(a) the construction of instruments and procedures for measurement; and

(*b*) the development and refinement of theoretical approaches to measurement.

Much of the early theoretical and applied work in psychometrics was undertaken in an attempt to measure intelligence. Francis Galton, often referred to as "the father of psychometrics", devised and included mental tests among his anthropometric measures. However, the origin of psychometrics also has connections to the related field of psychophysics. Two other pioneers of psychometrics obtained doctorates in the Leipzig Psychophysics Laboratory under Wilhelm Wundt: James McKeen Cattell in 1886 and Charles Spearman in 1906.

The psychometrician L. L. Thurstone, founder and first president of the Psychometric Society in 1936, developed and applied a theoretical approach to measurement referred to as the law of comparative judgement, an approach that has close connections to the psychophysical theory of Ernst Heinrich Weber and Gustav Fechner. In addition, Spearman and Thurstone both made important contributions to the theory and application of factor analysis, a statistical method developed and used extensively in psychometrics.

More recently, psychometric theory has been applied in the measurement of personality, attitudes, and beliefs, and academic achievement. Measurement of these unobservable phenomena is difficult, and much of the research and accumulated science in this discipline has been developed in an attempt to properly define and quantify such phenomena. Critics, including practitioners in the physical sciences and social activists, have argued that such definition and quantification is impossibly difficult, and that such measurements are often misused, such as with psychometric personality tests used in employment procedures.

DEFINITION OF MEASUREMENT IN PSYCHOLOGY

The definition of measurement in the social sciences has a long history. A currently widespread definition, proposed by Stanley Smith Stevens, is that measurement is "the assignment of numerals to objects or events according to some rule". This definition was introduced in the paper in which Stevens proposed four levels of measurement. Although widely adopted, this definition differs in important respects from the more classical definition of measurement adopted in the physical sciences, which is that measurement is the numerical estimation and expression of the magnitude of one quantity relative to another.

Indeed, Stevens's definition of measurement was put forward in response to the British Ferguson Committee, whose chair, A. Ferguson, was a physicist. The committee was appointed in 1932 by the British Association for the Advancement of Science to investigate the possibility of quantitatively estimating sensory events. Although its chair and other members were physicists, the committee also included several psychologists. The committee's report highlighted the importance of the definition of measurement. While Stevens's response was to propose a new definition, which has had considerable influence in the field, this was by no means the only response to the report. Another, notably different, response was to accept the classical definition, as reflected in the following statement:

> "Measurement in psychology and physics are in no sense different. Physicists can measure when they can find the operations by which they may meet the necessary criteria; psychologists have but to do the same. They need not worry about the mysterious differences between the meaning of measurement in the two sciences."

These divergent responses are reflected in alternative approaches to measurement. For example, methods based on covariance matrices are typically employed on the premise that numbers, such as raw scores derived from assessments, are measurements. Such approaches implicitly entail Stevens's definition of measurement, which requires only that numbers are assigned according to some rule. The main research task, then, is generally considered to be the discovery of associations between scores, and of factors posited to underlie such associations.

On the other hand, when measurement models such as the Rasch model are employed, numbers are not assigned based on a rule. Instead, in keeping with Reese's statement above, specific criteria for measurement are stated, and the goal is to construct procedures or operations that provide data that meet the relevant criteria. Measurements are estimated based on the models, and tests are conducted to ascertain whether the relevant criteria have been met.

INSTRUMENTS AND PROCEDURES

The first psychometric instruments were designed to measure the concept of intelligence. The best known historical approach involved the Stanford-Binet IQ test, developed originally by the French psychologist Alfred Binet. Intelligence tests are useful tools for various purposes. An alternative conception of intelligence is that cognitive capacities within individuals are a manifestation of a general component, or general intelligence factor, as well as cognitive capacity specific to a given domain.

Psychometrics is applied widely in educational assessment to measure abilities in domains such as reading, writing, and mathematics. The main approaches in applying tests in these domains have been Classical Test Theory and the more recent Item Response Theory and Rasch measurement models. These latter approaches permit joint scaling of persons and assessment items, which provides a basis for mapping of developmental continua by allowing descriptions of the skills displayed at various points along a continuum. Such approaches provide powerful information regarding the nature of developmental growth within various domains.

Another major focus in psychometrics has been on personality testing. There have been a range of theoretical approaches to conceptualizing and measuring personality. Some of the better known instruments include the Minnesota Multiphasic Personality Inventory, the Five-Factor Model and tools such as Personality and Preference Inventory and the Myers-Briggs Type Indicator. Attitudes have also been studied extensively using psychometric approaches. A common method in the measurement of attitudes is the use of the Likert scale. An alternative method involves the application of unfolding measurement models, the most general being the Hyperbolic Cosine Model.

THEORETICAL APPROACHES

Psychometricians have developed a number of different measurement theories. These include Classical Test Theory (CTT) and Item Response Theory (IRT) An approach which seems mathematically to be similar to IRT but also quite distinctive, in terms of its origins and features, is represented by the Rasch model for measurement. The development of the Rasch model, and the broader class of models to which it belongs, was explicitly founded on requirements of measurement in the physical sciences.

Psychometricians have also developed methods for working with large matrices of correlations and covariances. Techniques in this general tradition include:

factor analysis, a method of determining the underlying dimensions of data; multidimensional scaling, a method for finding a simple representation for data with a large number of latent dimensions; and data clustering, an approach to finding objects that are like each other. All these multivariate descriptive methods try to distill large amounts of data into simpler structures. More recently, structural equation modeling and path analysis represent more sophisticated approaches to working with large covariance matrices. These methods allow statistically sophisticated models to be fitted to data and tested to determine if they are adequate fits.

One of the main deficiencies in various factor analyses is a lack of consensus in cutting points for determining the number of latent factors. A usual procedure is to stop factoring when eigenvalues drop below one because the original sphere shrinks. The lack of the cutting points concerns other multivariate methods, also.

Key Concepts

Key concepts in classical test theory are reliability and validity. A reliable measure is one that measures a construct consistently across time, individuals, and situations. A valid measure is one that measures what it is intended to measure. A measure may be reliable without being valid. However, reliability is necessary, but not sufficient, for validity.

Both reliability and validity can be assessed statistically. Consistency over repeated measures of the same test can be assessed with the Pearson correlation coefficient, and is often called test-retest reliability. Similarly, the equivalence of different versions of the same measure can be indexed by a Pearson correlation, and is called equivalent forms reliability or a similar term.

Internal consistency, which addresses the homogeneity of a single test form, may be assessed by correlating performance on two halves of a test, which is termed split-half reliability; the value of this Pearson product-moment correlation coefficient for two half-tests is adjusted with the Spearman-Brown prediction formula to correspond to the correlation between two full-length tests. Perhaps the most commonly used index of reliability is Cronbach's a, which is equivalent to the mean of all possible split-half coefficients. Other approaches include the intra-class correlation, which is the ratio of variance of measurements of a given target to the variance of all targets.

There are a number of different forms of validity. Criterion-related validity can be assessed by correlating a measure with a criterion measure known to be valid. When the criterion measure is collected at the same time as the measure being validated the goal is to establish concurrent validity; when the criterion is collected later the goal is to establish predictive validity. A measure has construct validity if it is related to measures of other constructs as required by theory. Content validity is a demonstration that the items of a test are drawn from the domain being measured. In a personnel selection example, test content is based on a defined statement or set of statements of knowledge, skill, ability, or other characteristics obtained from a job analysis.

Item response theory models the relationship between latent traits and responses to test items. Among other advantages, IRT provides a basis for obtaining an estimate of the location of a test-taker on a given latent trait as well as the standard error of measurement of that location. For example, a university student's knowledge of history can be deduced from his or her score on a university test and then be compared reliably with a high school student's knowledge deduced from a less difficult test. Scores derived by classical test theory do not have this characteristic, and assessment of actual ability (rather than ability relative to other test-takers) must be assessed by comparing scores to those of a "norm group" randomly selected from the population. In fact, all measures derived from classical test theory are dependent on the sample tested, while, in principle, those derived from item response theory are not.

MEASUREMENT AND TESTING

Measurement is an essential component of the evaluation process. It is a critical part since resulting decisions are only as good as the data upon which the data are based. In general sense, data collection is involved in all phases of evaluation—the planning phase, the process phase and the product phase. Measurement, however, the process of quantifying the degree to which someone or something possesses a given trait, normally occurs in the process and the product phase.

Testing is necessary at certain points and useful at others. Testing can be conducted at the end of an instruction cycle—semester, term or unit. Such posttesting is for the purpose of determining the degree to which objectives (formal or informal) have been achieved, be they instructional objectives or programme objectives. Frequently, prettest or baseline data are collected at the beginning of the cycle. Prettests serve several purposes, the most important being that knowledge of the current status of a group may provide guidance for future activities as well as a basis of comparison for posttest results.

There are a variety of situations where testing is useful. A teacher may administer tests of entry behaviour to determine whether assumed pre-requisites have indeed been achieved. A special project designed to reduce dropouts may administer attitude tests and tests of personality variables such as introversion, aggression and anxiety in an effort to identify potential dropouts or to better understand students having difculties. A school may administer tests of scholastic aptitude in order to determine realistic achievement goals for students and to assist in the guidance process.

Data Collection

There are three major ways to collect data:

(a) administer a standardized instrument

(b) administer a locally developed instrument

(c) record naturally available data.

Depending upon the situation, one of these ways may be most appropriate or a combination may be required. Collection of available data, requiring minimum effort, sounds very attractive. There are not very many situations, however, for which this type of data is appropriate. Even when it is appropriate—that is, will facilitate intended decision making—there are problems inherent in this type of data. For example, the same letter grade does not necessarily represent the same level of achievement, even in two different classes in the same school or two different schools in the same system. Further, the records, for which the data are taken may be incomplete and disorganized. Developing an instrument for a particular purpose also has several major drawbacks. The development of a 'good' instrument requires considerable time, effort and skill. Training at least equivalent to a course in testing and evaluation is necessary in order to acquire the skills for good instrument development.

In contrast, the time it takes to select an appropriate instrument (usually from among standardized, commercially available instruments) is inevitably less than the time it takes to develop an instrument which measures the same thing. Further standardized instruments are typically developed by experts who possess the necessary skills. Tousands of standardized instruments are available which yield a wide variety of data for a wide variety of purposes. Major areas for which numerous measuring instruments have developed include achievement, personality and aptitude. Each of these can be in turn further divided into may subcategories. In general, it is usually a good idea to find out whether a suitable instrument is already available before jumping into instrument development. There are situations, however, for which use of available instruments is impractical or inappropriate. A teacher-made test, for example, is more appropriate or valid for assessing the degree to which students have achieved the objectives of a given unit.

Classification Schemes

At this point it must be emphasized that a test is not necessarily a written set of questions to which an individual responds in order to determine whether he/she passes. A more inclusive definition of a test is a means of measuring the knowledge, skills, feelings, intelligence or aptitude of an individual or a group. Tests produce numerical scores which can be used to identify, classify or otherwise evaluate test takers. While in practice most of tests are in paper-and-pencil form, there are many different kinds of tests and many different ways to classify them. The various classification schemes overlap considerably, and categories are by no means mutually exclusive. Any test can be classified on more than one dimension.

Response Behaviours

The term response behaviours refers to the way in which behaviours to be measured are exhibited. While in some cases responses to questions or other stimuli are given orally, usually, they are either written or take the form of an actual performance.

Written Responses

Written tests can be classified as either essays (subjective) or objective and standardized or locally-developed.

Essay vs Objective Tests:

(a) *Essays:* An essay test is one in which the number of questions is limited and responders must compose answers, typically lengthy, e.g., 'identify and discuss the major reforms in African education during the colonial period.' Determining the goodness or correctness of answers to such questions involves some degree of subjectivity.

(b) *Objective Tests:* An objective test is one for which subjectivity in scoring is eliminated, at least theoretically. In other words, anyone scoring a given test should come up with the same score. Examples of objective tests are multiple-choice tests, true-false tests, matching tests, and short answer tests.

Standardized vs. Locally Developed Tests:

(a) *Standardized Tests:* A standardized test is one that is developed by subject matter and measurement specialists, that is feld-tested under uniform administration procedures, that is revised to meet certain criteria and scored and interpreted using uniform procedures and standards. Standardization permeates all aspects of the test to the degree that it can be administered and scored exactly the same way every time it is given. Although other measurement instruments can be standardized, most standardized tests are objective, written tests requiring written responses. Although exceptions occur, the vast majority of standardized tests have been administered to groups referred to as the norm group. The performance of a norm group for a given test serves as the basis of comparison and interpretation for other groups to whom the test is administered. The score of a norm group are called norms. Ideally, the norm group is a large, well defined group which is representative of the group and subgroups for whom the test is intended.

(b) *Locally-developed Test*: The opposite of standardized test is obviously non-standardized test. Such tests are usually developed locally for a specific purpose. The tests used by teachers in the classroom are examples of locally-developed tests. Such tests do not have the characteristics of standardized tests. A locally-developed test may be as good as a standardized test, but not that often. Use of locally-developed test is usually more practical and more appropriate. A locally-developed test would more likely reffect what was actually taught in the classroom to a greater degree than standardized tests.

Performance Tests

For may objectives and areas of learning, use of written tests is inappropriate way of measuring behaviour. You cannot determine how well a student can type a letter, for example, with a multiple choice test or open question. Performance is one of these areas. Performance can take the form of a procedure or a product. A procedure is a series of steps, usually in a definite order, executed in performing an act or a task. Examples include, adjusting a microscope, passing a football, setting margins on type writer, drawing geometric fgures or calculating sum of fgures in Excel. A product is a tangible outcome or result. Examples of a product include typed letter, a painting, a poem, and a science project. In either case the performance is observed and rated in some way. Thus, performance is one which requires the execution of an act or the development of a product in order to determine whether or to what degree a given ability or trait exists.

Data Collection Methods: There are many different ways to collect data and classifying data collection methods is not easy. However, a logical way to categorize them initially is in terms of whether the data are obtained through self-report or observation.

(a) *Self-Report*. Self-report data consist of oral or written responses from individuals. An obvious type of self-report data is that resulting from the administration of standardized or locally-developed written tests, including certain achievement, personality and aptitude tests. Another type of self-report measure used in certain evaluation efforts is the questionnaire, an instrument with which you are probably familiar. Also, interviews are sometimes used.

(b) *Observation*. When observation is used, data are collected not by asking but by observing. A person being observed usually does not write anything; he or she does something and that behaviour is observed and recorded. For certain evaluation questions, observation is clearly the most appropriate approach. To use an example, you could ask students about their sportsmanship and you could ask teachers how they handle behaviour problems, but more objective information would probably would be obtained by actually observing students at sporting events and teacher in their classrooms. Two types of observation which are used in evaluation efforts are natural observation and observation of simulation. Certain kinds of behaviours can only be observed as they occur naturally. In such situations, the observer does not control or manipulate anything, and in fact works very hard at not affecting the observed situation in any way. As an example, classroom behaviour can best be addressed through observation. In simulation observation, the evaluator creates the situation to be observed and tells participants what activities they are to engage in. This technique allows the evaluator to observe behaviour which occurs infrequently in natural situations or not at all.

(c) *Rating Scale.* Is an instrument with a number of items related to a given variable, each item representing a continuum of categories between two extremes; persons responding to items place a mark to indicate their position on each item. Rating scales can be used as self-report or as n observation instrument, depending on the purpose for which they are used.

Behaviours Measured: Virtually all possible behaviours that can be measured fall into one of three major categories: achievement, character and personality, and aptitude. All of these can be standardized or locally-developed. These categories also apply equally well to the three domains of educational outcome, namely cognitive, affective an psychomotor.

(a) *Achievement.* Achievement tests measure the correct status of individuals with respect to prof-ciency in given areas of knowledge or skills. Achievement tests are appropriate for many types of evaluation besides individual student evaluation. Achievement test can be standardized (which are designed to cover content which are common to many classes of the same type) or locally-developed (designed to measure particular set of learning outcomes, set by specific teacher). Standardized tests are, in turn, available for individual curriculum areas or in the form of batteries, which measure achievement in several different areas.

A diagnostic test is a type of achievement test which yields multiple scores for each area of achievement; these scores facilitate identification of specific areas or defciency or learning difculty. Items in a diagnostic test are intended to identify skills and knowledge that students must have achieved before they proceed to another level. Ideally, diagnosis should be an ongoing process and the teacher must design them in a way that such tests help him/her find out the problems that students encounter as they proceed in the learning process.

(b) *Character and Personality.* Tests of character and personality are designed to measure characteristics of individuals along a number of dimensions and to assess feelings and attitudes toward self, others, and a variety of activities, institutions and situations. Most of the tests of character and personality are self-report measures and ask an individual to respond to a series of questions or statements. There are instruments in this category which are designed to measure personality, attitudes, creativity, and interest of students.

(c) *Aptitude.* Aptitude tests are measures of potential. They are used to predict how well someone is likely to perform in a future situation. Tests of general aptitude are variously referred to as scholastic aptitude tests, intelligence tests, and tests of general mental ability. Aptitude tests are also available to predict a person's likely level of performance after following some specific future instruction or training. Aptitude tests are available in the form of individual test on specific subject or content or in the form of batteries. While virtually all aptitude tests are standardized and administered as part of school testing programme, the results are useful to teachers, counsellors and administrators. Readiness aptitude tests are administered prior to instruction or training in a specific area in order to determine whether and to what degree a student is ready for, or will proft from, an instruction. Readiness tests, which are part of aptitude tests, typically include measurement of variables such as auditory discrimination, visual discrimination and motor ability.

Performance Standards: Performance standards are the criteria to which the results of measurement are compared in order to interpret them. A test score in and of itself means nothing. If I tell you that Shetty got 18 correct, what does that tell you about Shetty's performance? Absolutely nothing. Now if I tell that the average score for the test was 15, at least you know that he did better than the average. If instead I tell you that a score of 17 was required for a master classification, you don't know anything about the performance of the rest of the class, but you know that Shetty attained mastery. These are the two ways with which we can interpret the results of a test, first by comparing it to other students in the class or by comparing it to a pre-determined criteria.

Norm-referenced Standards: Any test, standardized or locally-developed, which reports and interprets each score in terms of its relative position with respect to other scores on the same test, is norm-referenced. If your total IQ score is 100, for example, the interpretation is that your measured intelligence is average, average compared to scores of a norm group. The raw scores resulting from administration of standardized test are converted to some other index which indicates relative position. One such equivalent technique familiar to you is the percentile. A given percentile indicates the percentage of the scores that were lower than the percentile's corresponding score. For example, Mr. Shetty might have scored on the 42nd percentile in a standardized math test, that means 42 per cent of the students who took that test scored below Shettyd. In such way of communicating student scores, there is no indication of what Mr. Shetty knows or does not know. The only interpretation are in terms of Shetty's achievement compared to the achievement of others.

Norm-referenced tests are based on the assumption that measured traits involve normal curve properties. The idea of the normal curve is that measured traits exist in different amounts in different people. Some people have a lot of it, some people have little of it, and most have some amount called the 'average' amount. For example, if you administer a math test to a class of 100 students, given that the test of appropriate level—that is not too easy nor too low—a small portion of the class will perform high and another equal portion will perform low, while the majority will perform around the average score. The normal curve is figured below.

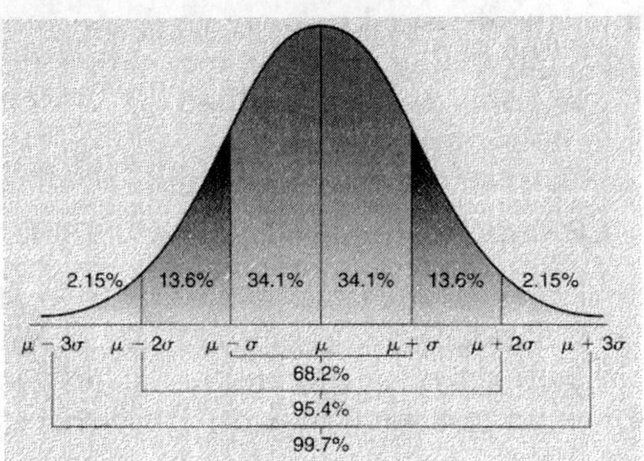

Most of the scores are (the highest frequency) are average, fewer scores are above or below average, and very few are way above or way below the average. The average group contains approximately 65 per cent of the scores. Norm-referenced measurement is used in this hypothetical distribution of scores is applied to real classroom or assessment situations. That is, when the top 2-3 per cent are given As (whatever their scores be), the next 15 per cent are given Bs, the next 65 per cent receive Cs, the next 15 per cent are given D, and the bottom 2-3 per cent receive F grades. The letter grades are assigned irrespective of the actual performance of the student.

There is one problem with norm-referenced standards. Some people can get good grades (or conversely bad grades) without necessarily exhibiting the corresponding performance level. Such method may encourage the students, but it may cause a special problem when the class is more homogeneous.

Criterion-referenced Standards

Any test which reports and interprets each score in terms of an absolute standard is criterion-referenced. In other words, interpretation of one person's score has nothing to do with anybody's score. A score is compared with a standard or performance, not with scores of other people. When criterion-referenced tests are used, everyone taking the test may do well or everyone may do poorly. In this context, criterion can be defined as a domain of behaviours measuring an objective.

CHARACTERISTICS OF A GOOD TEST

There are a number of characteristics which are desirable for all tests. Standardized tests, which are developed by experts in both subject matter and evaluation, are more likely to live up to these standards. These characteristics, which are discussed in a more detailed manner, include;

(*a*) Test objectivity
(*b*) Discrimination
(*c*) Comprehensiveness
(*d*) Validity
(*e*) Reliability
(*f*) Specification of conditions of administering
(*g*) Direction of scoring and interpretation

Test Objectivity

Test objectivity means that an individual's score is the same, or essentially the same, regardless of who is doing the scoring. A test is objective when instructor opinion, bias, or individual judgement is not a major factor in scoring. Tests may be scored by more than one person, at different or the same time. In education, we wonder to what extent is the scoring of these individual scorers is the same. If the possible difference between the people scoring the same test high, that test is low in objectivity. Tough individual's may naturally be different in the way they perceive information, we assume that the more objective a test is, the more aspires to the high quality evaluation we all envision in education. This does not mean that tests which do not have high degree of objectivity are not of quality. Even subjective tests, though they are designed to measure information that can be looked at from different angles, certain level of objectivity is necessary. The individual designing must have something in mind that constitutes good performance on such test. Tat thing can be multiple, but criteria must be developed to make sure any scoring is fair enough to contribute to discriminating of students on such basis. Objectivity is a relative term.

Discrimination

The test should be constructed in such a manner that it

will detect or measure small differences in achievement or attainment. This is essential if the test is to be used for ranking students on the basis of individual achievement or for assigning grades. It is not an important consideration if the test is used to measure the level of the entire class or as an instructional quiz where the primary purpose is instruction rather than measurement. As is true with validity, reliability, and objectivity, the discriminating power of a test is increased by concentrating on and improving each individual test item. After the test has been administered, an item analysis can be made that will show the relative difculty of each item and the extent to which each discriminates between good and poor students. Often, as in obtaining reliability, it is necessary to increase the length of the test to get clear-cut discrimination. A discriminating test:

(a) Produces a wide range of scores when administered to the students who have signifcantly different achievements.

(b) Will include items at all levels of difculty. Some items will be answered correctly only by the best students; others will be relatively easy and will be answered correctly by most students. If all students answer an item correctly, it lacks discrimination.

Comprehensiveness

For a test to be comprehensive, it should sample major lesson objectives. It is neither necessary nor practical to test every objective that is taught in a course, but a sufcient number of objectives should be included to provide a valid measure of student achievement in the complete course.

Validity

The most important characteristic of a good examination

is validity; that is, the extent to which a test measures what it is intended to measure. It is vital for a test to be valid in order for the results to be accurately applied and interpreted.

Validity isn't determined by a single statistic, but by a body of research that demonstrates the relationship between the test and the behaviour it is intended to measure. There are three types of validity:

(a) Content Validity

When a test has content validity, the items on the test represent the entire range of possible items the test should cover. Individual test questions may be drawn from a large pool of items that cover a broad range of topics.

In some instances where a test measures a trait that is difficult to define, an expert judge may rate each item's relevance. Because each judge is basing their rating on opinion, two independent judges rate the test separately. Items that are rated as strongly relevant by both judges will be included in the final test.

(b) Criterion-related Validity

A test is said to have criterion-related validity when the test is demonstrated to be effective in predicting criterion or indicators of a construct. There are two different types of criterion validity:

– *Concurrent Validity* occurs when the criterion measures are obtained at the same time as the test scores. This indicates the extent to which the test scores accurately estimate an individual's current state with regards to the criterion. For example, on a test that measures levels of depression, the test would be said to have concurrent validity if it measured the current levels of depression experienced by the test-taker.

– *Predictive Validity* occurs when the criterion measures are obtained at a time after the test. Examples of test with predictive validity are career or aptitude tests, which are helpful in determining who is likely to succeed or fail in certain subjects or occupations.

(c) Construct Validity

A test has construct validity if it demonstrates an association between the test scores and the prediction of a theoretical trait. Intelligence tests are one example of measurement instruments that should have construct validity.

The instructor can ensure whether his/her test items are valid by following accepted test construction procedures that include:

(a) Use of the lesson objectives as a basis for the test requirements. An examination so constructed will tend to measure what has been taught.

(b) Review of the test items and the completed examination by other instructors.

(c) Selection of the most appropriate form of test and type of test item. Thus, if the instructor desires to measure "ability to do," he must select that form of the test that will require the student to demonstrate his "ability to do." If another less desirable form is used, it must be recognized that the validity of the measurement has been reduced.

(d) Presentation of test requirements in a clear and unambiguous manner. If the test material cannot be interpreted accurately by the student, he or she will not realize what is being covered; hence, he or she will be unable to respond as anticipated. Such a test cannot be valid.

(e) Elimination, so far as is possible, of those factors that are not related to the measurement of the

teaching pints. A test that is not within the capabilities of the students as to time or educational level may fail to measure their actual learning in the course.

Reliability

Reliability refers to the consistency of a measure. A test is considered reliable if we get the same result repeatedly. For example, if a test is designed to measure a trait (such as introversion), then each time the test is administered to a subject, the results should be approximately the same. Unfortunately, it is impossible to calculate reliability exactly, but there several different ways to estimate reliability.

(a) Test-Retest Reliability

To gauge test-retest reliability, the test is administered twice at two different points in time. This kind of reliability is used to assess the consistency of a test across time. This type of reliability assumes that there will be no change in the quality or construct being measured. Test-retest reliability is best used for things that are stable over time, such as intelligence. Generally, reliability will be higher when little time has passed between tests.

(b) Inter-ratter Reliability

This type of reliability is assessed by having two or more independent judges score the test. The scores are then compared to determine the consistency of the ratters estimates. One way to test inter-ratter reliability is to have each ratter assign each test item a score. For example, each ratter might score items on a scale from 1 to 10. Next, you would calculate the correlation between the two rating to determine the level of inter-ratter reliability. Another means of testing inter-ratter reliability is to have ratters determine which category each observations falls into and then calculate the percentage of agreement between the ratters. So, if the ratters agree 8 out of 10 times, the test has an 80 per cent inter-ratter reliability rate.

(c) Parallel-Forms Reliability

Parallel-forms reliability is gauged by comparing to different tests that were created using the same content. This is accomplished by creating a large pool of test items that measure the same quality and then randomly dividing the items into two separate tests. The two tests should then be administered to the same subjects at the same time.

(d) Internal Consistency Reliability

This form of reliability is used to judge the consistency of results across items on the same test. Essentially, -you are comparing test items that measure the same construct to determine the tests internal consistency. When you see a question that seems very similar to another test question, it may indicate that the two questions are being used to gauge reliability. Because the two questions are similar and designed to measure the same thing, the test taker should answer both questions the same, which would indicate that the test has internal consistency.

The following factors will infuence the reliability of a test:

(a) Administration. It is essential that each student have the same time, equipment, instructions, assistance, and examination environment. Test directions should be strictly enforced.

(b) Scoring. Objectivity in scoring contributes to reliability. Every effort should be made to obtain uniformity of scoring standards and practices.

(c) Standards. The standards of performance that are established for one class should be consistent with those used in other classes. A change in grading

policies not based upon facts, uniform standards, and experience factors gained from other classes will affect the reliability of test results.

(d) *Instruction.* The reliability of tests results will be affected if the instruction presented to a class tends to overemphasize the teaching points included in the examination. This is often known as "teaching the test" and is undesirable. When the instructor gives students obvious clues as to the test requirements, he not only affects the reliability of the test, but he insults the intelligence of his class.

(e) *Length.* The more responses required of students, the more reliable will be the test or measuring device.

Specification of Conditions of Administration

A good test must specify the conditions under which the test must be conducted. The conditions must give all students a fair chance to show what their performance. This will improve the reliability of the test. Standardized must come along with specification on the conditions in which students must perform. Administering the test with highly varied conditions will highly interfere with the results of the test. In general, when administering a test, the following must be kept in mind:

(a) *Physical conditions*:
- Light, ventilation, quiet, etc.

(b) *Psychological conditions:*
- Avoid inducing test anxiety
- Try to reduce test anxiety
- Don't give test when other events will distract

(c) *Suggestions*:
- Don't talk unnecessarily before the test

- Minimize interruptions
- Don't give hints to individuals who ask about items
- Discourage cheating
- Give students equal time to take the test.

Direction for Scoring and Interpreting Test Results

Good test must come with direction on how to score and interpret the results of a test. This is specially important for standardized tests, which are used by individuals other than those who developed the test in the first place. Such directions are also important for locally-developed tests, since other individuals may get involved in the process of scoring and interpreting the test, due to unforeseen circumstances.

The following guidelines contribute to the development of clear direction for tests.

(*a*) Provide clear descriptions of detailed procedures for administering tests in a standardized manner.

(*b*) Provide information to test takers or test users on test question formats and procedures for answering test questions, including information on the use of any needed materials and equipment.

(*c*) Establish and implement procedures to ensure the security of testing materials during all phases of test development, administration, scoring, and reporting.

(*d*) Provide procedures, materials and guidelines for scoring the tests, and for monitoring the accuracy of the scoring process. If scoring the test is the responsibility of the test developer, provide adequate training for scorers.

(*e*) Correct errors that affect the interpretation of the scores and communicate the corrected results promptly.

(*f*) Develop and implement procedures for ensuring the confdentiality of scores.

SELECTION OF A TEST

Usually, when we talk of selection of measuring instruments or tests, we are referring to standardized instruments. In most of the situations, you may have only one option you are compelled to choose. However, in some cases, you may be confronted with the challenge of comparing instruments and choosing the one that best suits your needs and circumstances. In such scenario, you must be your decision on objective facts and sound evaluation principles.

First and foremost, you have to think of the measurement technique that meets the purpose of the testing and the objectives to be measured. For example, the evaluation plan for an experimental reading curriculum would involve a combination of locally-developed and standardized instruments. It may also involve both norm-referenced and criterion-referenced formats. On the other hand, school testing programme would require the sole use of standardized tests.

When you are required to select a standardized test from a number of options, you also need to consider the following factors completeness of the information concerning characteristics of the test. Surprisingly, there is a relationship between the amount of information supplied by the publisher and the quality of the test. The most important information required is the validity of the test. In addition, data concerning the reliability of the test should be available and meet the standards we set for our testing exercise. Other data which should be reported include information concerning test administration, scoring and interpretation.

DESIGNING A TEST

Restriction, Definition and Selection of Content

The first step in designing a test is to put boundaries on what is to be covered in a test. Objectives usually provide the blueprint for the topics or clusters of topics to be included in a test, and a test should represent meaningful unit of instruction. A test will normally represent a range from several days to several weeks of instruction. Narrowing test coverage prevents cognitive overload on the part of students, and permits a large more representative sampling of the behaviours represented by the selected objectives. Of course, certain cumulative tests such final exams require broader coverage and may represent weeks or even months of instruction. If individual tests have been carefully designed, the task of developing cumulative tests is facilitated since the outcomes measured by such tests represent a sampling of the performances measured on all previous tests.

The next thing in designing a test is to make a detailed content outline (or syllabuses) if such is not already available. The outline needs to be detailed enough to include knowledge and skill outcomes desired of students. While each and every outcome may not be measured on a test, they should all at least be candidates for inclusion. If specific objectives have been formulated, then desired performances associated with each entry in the outline will already be specified. If not these behaviours now have to be identified, and we must keep in mind that we are concerned with more than just the possession of knowledge. This process of content description is called 'domain description' and is intended to identify all possible items by delineating rules for generating items.

The third step in designing a test is to devise a scheme for sampling from the domain of behaviours.

With the exception of certain mastery tests, a test invariably represents a sample of behaviours. It is just not possible to measure each and every aspect of each and every outcome. Further, if we carefully select the ones we really measure, we can generalize to the total domain with a reasonable degree of confdence. It is a requirement that test items constitute a representative sample of desired behaviours. This is what we have called content validity. The more structured and well-defined the content is, the easier this is to accomplish. Random selection, which gives each outcome an independent and equal chance of being included in the test, leads to the process of attaining content validity in a test. You can also select the outcomes to be selected for the test by stratifying the content on the basis of criteria inherent to the content (or some other logical criteria).

One systematic approach to test design is involves the development of a table of specifications. Once test content has been identified and defined, and all the behavioural outcomes specified, a logical next step is the construction of a table of specifications.

Table of Specifications

A table of specification is essentially a blueprint for a test. At the name implies, it specified the content of the test. Its basic purpose is to insure that all intended outcomes, and only the intended outcomes, are measured and that the test includes the appropriate number of items for each measured item. A table of specification is a two-way table with one axis being essentially a content outline and the other axis indicating the behaviours desired with respect to content.

Content outline

Along one axis of the table of specifications, the major headings and subheadings of the content outline are listed. The table of specifications may include all topics and subtopics, or it may include only those that have been specially specified. The more detailed this axis is, the more likely it is that the test will include items for all desired topics. Also, to greater extent, the complexity of the outline is a function of the complexity of the content area being measured.

Behavioural outcomes

Along the axis of the table the behaviours or performances for each topic are given. This approach focuses attention on higher order outcomes and insures that the test will not contain predominantly or totally knowledge level items. The level of the items will mainly depend on the level of students and the objectives already set. However, it should be noted that teachers are more likely to neglect items that measure higher order skills, such application, synthesis and analysis. Some tables of specifications may go as specific indicating the sub-domain the outcome is related to. It should be noted that it is easier to develop table of specifications for criterion-referenced tests than for norm-referenced tests, since intended outcomes for the former have already been thought through and delineated.

Number of items

The intersection of content outline headings and behavioural outcome categories forms cells into which appropriate number (or percentage) of items is placed. The number of items allocated for each cell should be based on the number of objectives or their weight (or importance). This means, we have to think thoroughly about 'what it takes' to measure a particular behavioural outcome for a given topic.

Developing a table of specifications is a planning activity and ideally should be executed during the planning phase of evaluation. The logical time to do so is soon after developing specific objectives. If objectives are laid out for an entire term, a logical next step is to divide them into sets representing manageable units of instruction. As with objectives, if developed prior to instruction, a table of specifications serves as a guide for instruction since we know what outcomes are intended for what topics, and the desired emphasis to be placed on each.

Constructing Test Items

There are a number of guidelines for developing a number of different types of items. When students read an item, we want the only factor affecting whether they answer it correctly to be whether they possess the behaviour being measured, that is, whether they have achieved the objective. And yet, there are a number of characteristics of an item that can either prevent knowledgeable student from getting it correct or permit a unknowledgeable student to get it correct. Factors such as the way a question is worded, the nature of the alternatives, and the directions for responding can affect a students' ability to demonstrate a student achievement or lack of it.

There are basically two types of test items, essay and objective. Objective items include short answer, multiple choice, true false, and matching. Test items can also be classified as supply or selection items. Essay and short answer items are supply items because the answer must be supplied by the student. Multiple choice, true and false and matching items are referred to as selection items since the student selects an answer among provided alternatives. Which item type or types are appropriate for a given test depends mostly upon the nature of behaviours being measured and the nature of instruction. There are no item types that are specific for some specific kind of outcomes; any item type can be used to measure any behavioural outcome regardless of its taxonomy level.

General Guidelines

It is generally recommended against the development of a test in a hurry. The teacher, or the person responsible the evaluation, should get enough time to plan, develop and revise items. Certain tests, such as posts, must be developed prior to instruction. Unit tests, on the other hand, can be developed following instruction. It is advisable to develop tests ahead of time and revise as necessary, or you can develop the test as you go along. This approach has a number of advantages, the most important being the fact that it spreads the difculty task of test construction over a period of time.

Items should directly correspond to with the intended behavioural outcome or objective. In other words, the behaviour elicited by the item should be precisely the behaviour specified in the objective. If an objective states that the student should be able handle microscope, the corresponding item should not ask him/her to list the parts of a microscope or its uses; rather, it should require students to handle it. This is called objective—item correspondence.

Closely related to the concept of objective-item correspondence is the item sufciency. Item sufciency means that a correct response to an item (or items) constitutes sufcient evidence that the student has demonstrated the intended behaviour, or has achieved the objective. Depending upon the nature of the objective, it might not be possible to develop such an item; several items may well be required to meet the sufciency guideline. It is, however, a goal to work toward.

One major requirement of an item is that it should clearly communicate to the test takers the meaning intended by the test developer. In other words, the item should be as free from ambiguity as possible. The way the student interpreted the item should be the way the test developer intended it to be interpreted. The item should also clearly communicate to any competent scorer.

Item difculty is an item characteristic that can be manipulated by the test developer. Appropriate levels of difculty are a function of both the type of test and the objectives upon which the test is based. In any case, test developers should balance item difculty by including items from all levels of the continuum.

Item novelty is a concept that applies to primarily to measurement of higher-order outcomes. It refers to conditions where the situation in the item is one that is totally unfamiliar to the student, that is, one that was not previously encountered during instruction. If this condition is not met, an item that is intended to measure high order outcome may in fact be a knowledge item.

Essay Tests

Essay tests are primarily used by teachers for student evaluation. Some standardized tests do contain essay items, and a formal evaluation effort may occasionally utilize such items but their use is generally confned to the classroom. An essay test is one which contains items which require the student to compose responses, usually lengthy ones. Essay test is appropriate for measuring outcomes that involve high-order skills, such as application and synthesis. It should be noted that the scoring of objectives tests is generally subjective. This means that there is no only one and answer; but there can be a number of alternative ways that would correctly answer the question involved. Because essay responses are lengthier than those of objective tests, fewer questions can be asked in a given amount of time.

Objective items are more difficult to construct but easier to score; essay tests, on the other hand, are tough to score but relatively easy to construct. The general guidelines for item construction—objective-item correspondence, sufciency, communication, difculty and novelty—apply with special emphasis on communication, since there are no response alternatives to help clarify the question, it is crucial that the desired response alternatives be delineated as clearly as possible. Students should be instruction on what is required and how the question should be answered. In addition, students should be given general guidelines concerning length, time and scoring.

As already indicated, the scoring of essay tests is difficult and time-consuming process. While it is potentially a very subjective process involving low scorer reliability, the degree of subjectivity can be considerably minimized by carefully planning and scoring. We can objectify essay tests to the degree that we can specify appropriate responses and alternative acceptable responses, then any knowledgeable scorer should be able to determine whether the responses are there. There are two basic approaches to the process of scoring essay tests, the analytical method and the global method.

(a) The analytical approach involves identifying all the aspects or components of a perfect answer and assigning a point value to each.

(b) The global method, also referred to as the rating method or the holistic approach, results in more subjective, less reliable scoring, but it takes less time. It involves identifying all the aspects of or components of a perfect answer, but point values are not assigned to each; instead, each response is judged as a whole, a total unit, and an overall rating is made. Based, on the perceived completeness of the responses, points are assigned.

As a general guideline for essay tests, it is recommended to score each response without knowledge of who wrote it, that is anonymously. This prevents scores being biased by extraneous factors, such as feelings about individual students. It is also good idea to read and score essay questions twice, before points are assigned. Ideally, this should be done by two different persons.

Objective Tests

Objective tests, in which students are not required to compose responses but rather to select from among a number of given alternatives, are more valid and reliable than essay items, and scorer reliability is much higher. Objective tests can be used to measure objectives at all levels, and are not confned to knowledge level items, as argued by many. The general guidelines for item construction, which we have previously discussed generally apply. The following recommendations can help you avoid common pitfalls.

- *(a)* Be careful not to provide clues to the right answer.
- *(b)* Dependent items (when correct answer for one item is necessary in order to answer another item) should be avoided.
- *(c)* Irrelevant difculty should not be promoted, either intentionally or unintentionally, by using complex vocabulary or by making the item more complicated than it needs to be.
- *(d)* Avoid negatives, specially double negatives.
- *(e)* Direct quotes should be avoided.
- *(f)* Trivia should not be measured.
- *(g)* An item should have only one correct or best answer, unless otherwise specified.

Objective items include:

- *(a)* Short answer items
- *(b)* Multiple choice items

(*c*) True-false items

(*d*) Matching items

General Guidelines for the Organization, Directions and Format of Tests

Organization of Tests Items

- If there is one type of item, items of the same type should be together.
- Items can also be arranged on a continuum, from least difficult to most difcult.
- Another logical way to arrange items is by subject matter topic. All items related to the same objective or outcome should be grouped together.

General Directions

- If the purpose and importance of the test are not self-evident, they should be discussed with the students in order to orient them and motivate them to do their best.
- In additions to directions for selecting (or supplying) answers, students should be instructed as how to record the answers.
- If directions are complicated, or involve procedures unfamiliar to the students, an example or sample item should be presented to the students.
- It is good idea that the test take develops scorer key.
- If some topics are more important than others, it is better to have more items for these topics than to assign some items a higher value.
- If test taking time is not ample, students should be given some guidelines for using their time effectively.

- If there is not penalty for guessing, students should be encouraged to answer every item, even if are not sure of the correct answer.
- If there is penalty for guessing, students should be instructed to respond only to those items for which are reasonably sure concerning the correct answer.

Format Considerations

- Items should be numbered consecutively, and directions should be prominently positioned and separated from the actual items.
- Answer spaces should be of equal size and large enough to accommodate the longest response, especially on short-answer tests, and answer spaces should be placed in a vertical column in the right or left hand margin or a separate answer sheet may be used.
- If an item is accompanied by any type of illustration, such as diagrams, it should be accurate and placed adjacent to the item, directly above it if possible or parallel to it.

Test Revision

Test revision may actually occur prior to its intended use as well as following its formal administration. Instruments developed for specific, formal evaluation may be administered and revised over and over again until acceptable levels of validity and reliability are achieved. The process is called feldtesting or test validation.

3

Patterns of Evaluation and Measurement in Education System

Education aims at making children capable of becoming responsible, productive and useful members of a society. Knowledge, skills and attitudes are built through learning experiences and opportunities created for learners in school. It is in the classroom that learners can analyse and evaluate their experiences, learn to doubt, to question, to investigate and to think independently. The aim of education simultaneously reflects the current needs and aspirations of a society as well as its lasting values and human ideals. At any given time and place it can be called the contemporary and contextual articulations of broad and lasting human aspirations and values.

An understanding of learners, educational aims, the nature of knowledge, and the nature of the school as a social organization can help us arrive at principles to guide classroom practices. Conceptual development is thus a continuous process of deepening and enriching connections and acquiring new layers of meaning. Simultaneously theories that children have about the natural and social world, develop, including about themselves in relation to others, which provide them with explanations for why things are the way they are and the relationship between the cause and its effect. Attitudes, emotions and values are thus an integral part of cognitive development, and are linked to the development of language, mental representations, concepts and reasoning. As children's metacognitive capabilities develop, they become more aware of their own beliefs and capable of regulating their own learning.

Examinations are an indispensable part of the educational process as some form of assessment is necessary to determine the effectiveness of teaching learning process and their internalization by learners. Various Commissions and Committees have felt the need for examination reforms. The Hunter Commission (1882), Calcutta University Commission or Sadler Commission (1917-1919), Hartog Committee Report (1929), the Report of Central Advisory Board or Sargeant Plan (1944), Secondary Education Commission or Mudaliar Commission (1952-53) have all made recommendations regarding reducing emphasis on external examination and encouraging internal assessment through Continuous and Comprehensive Evaluation.

The need for Continuous and Comprehensive School Based Evaluation has been reiterated over the last few decades. The Kothari Commission report (1966) observed, 'On the completion of the course, at the end of the lower or higher secondary stage, the student should receive a certificate from the school also giving the record of his internal assessment as contained in his cumulative record. This certificate may be attached to that given by the Board in connection with the external examination...'. It further adds, 'This internal assessment or evaluation conducted by the schools is of greater significance and should be given increasing importance. It should be comprehensive, evaluating all those aspects of students' growth that are measured by the external examination and also those personality traits, interests and attitudes which cannot be assessed by it.'

This aspect has been strongly taken care of in the National Policy on Education (1986) which states that "Continuous and Comprehensive Evaluation that incorporates both scholastic and non-scholastic aspects of evaluation, spread over the total span of instructional time" should be followed.

Report on the Committee for Review of NPE (1986) recommendation brought out by Government of India in 1991 lays down norms for "continuous comprehensive internal evaluation and suggests safeguards against abuse of this evaluation system".

Report on the CABE Committee on Policy brought out by Ministry of Human Resource Development (MHRD), Govt. of India in January, 1992 has also referred to the provisions of NPE with regard to evaluation process and examination reforms and also suggested 'continuous and comprehensive internal evaluation of the scholastic and non-scholastic achievement of the students'

The Report of the Task Force on the Role and status of the Board of Secondary Education (1997) observed: In our scheme of things, it is the School Boards which are expected to play the central role in the academic renovation of the school system. In other words, leadership has to come from the Board. Once the Boards get committed to this vital and supplementary system of evaluation and push it vigorously, this innovation will come to be accepted by more and more schools.

PLACE OF EVALUATION IN CURRICULUM

A curriculum is what constitutes a total teaching-learning program comprising overall aims, syllabus, materials, methods and assessment. In short it provides a framework of knowledge and capabilities, seen as appropriate to a particular level. Evaluation not only measures the progress and achievement of the learners but also the effectiveness of the teaching materials and methods used for transaction. Hence, evaluation should be viewed as a component of curriculum with the twin purpose of effective delivery and further improvement in the teaching learning process.

If properly understood, evaluation or assessment will not be perceived as something administered by the teachers and taken by the learners on the conclusion of a period of learning. When evaluation is seen as an end of the learning exercise, both the teachers and the learners will tend to keep it outside the teaching-learning process, rendering assessment broadly irrelevant and alien to the curriculum. Further, such a perception associates anxiety and stress with evaluation for learners. On the contrary, if evaluation is seen as an integral part built into the teaching learning process; learners will not perceive tests and examination with fear. It will lead to diagnosis, remedial action and enhancement of learning.

The scope of evaluation in schools extends to almost all the areas of learners' personality development. It should include both scholastic and co-scholastic areas, i.e. it should be *comprehensive* in nature. This is in line with the goals of education. Evaluation is continuous and reveals the strengths and weaknesses of learners more frequently, so that the learners have better opportunity to understand and improve themselves. It also provides feedback to the teachers for modifying their teaching strategies. In view of getting a complete picture of the child's learning, assessment should focus on the learner's ability to:

- Learn and acquire desired skills related to different subject areas
- Acquire a level of achievement in different subject areas in the requisite measure

- Develop child's individual skills, interests, attitudes and motivation
- Understand and lead a healthy and productive life
- Monitor the changes taking place in child's learning, behaviour and progress over a period of time
- Respond to different situations and opportunities both in and out of school
- Apply what is learnt in a variety of environment, circumstances and situations
- Work independently, collaboratively and harmoniously
- Analyze and evaluate
- Be aware of social and environmental issues
- Participate in social and environmental projects
- Retain what is learned over a period of time

Thus assessment is a useful, desirable and an enabling process. To realize this, one needs to keep the following parameters in mind.

Assessment needs to:

- Use a variety of ways to collect information about the learner's learning and progress in all subjects
- Collect information continuously and record the same
- Give importance to each learner's way of responding and learning and time it takes to do so
- Report on a continuous basis and be sensitive to every learner's response
- Provide feedback that will lead to positive action and help the learner to do better

In the assessment process, one should be careful not to:

— Label learners as slow, poor, intelligent etc.
— Make comparisons between them
— Make negative statements

CONTINUOUS AND COMPREHENSIVE EVALUATION

Continuous and Comprehensive Evaluation (CCE) refers to a system of school based evaluation of a student that covers all aspects of a student development. It is a developmental process of student which emphasizes on two fold objectives. These objectives are continuity in evaluation and assessment of broad based learning and behaviourial outcomes on the other.

The term 'continuous' is meant to emphasise that evaluation of identified aspects of students 'growth and development' is a continuous process rather than an event, built into the total teaching-learning process and spread over the entire span of academic session. It means regularity of assessment frequency of unit testing, diagnosis of learning gaps, use of corrective measures, retesting and feedback of evidence to teachers and students for their self evaluation.

The second term 'comprehensive' means that the scheme attempts to cover both the scholastic and the co-scholastic aspects of the students' growth and development. Since abilities, attitudes and aptitudes can manifest themselves in forms other than the written word, the term refers to application of variety of tools and techniques (both testing and non-testing) and aims at assessing a learner's development in areas of learning, like:

(*a*) Knowledge
(*b*) Understanding
(*c*) Applying
(*d*) Analyzing

(*e*) Evaluating

(*f*) Creating

Objectives

The objectives of continuous and comprehensive evaluation are:

- To help develop cognitive, psychomotor and affective skills.
- To lay emphasis on thought process and de-emphasise memorization.
- To make evaluation an integral part of teaching-learning process.
- To use evaluation for improvement of students achievement and teaching-learning strategies on the basis of regular diagnosis followed by remedial instructions.
- To use evaluation as a quality control device to maintain desired standard of performance.
- To determine social utility, desirability or effectiveness of a programme and take appropriate decisions about the learner, the process of learning and the learning environment.
- To make the process of teaching and learning a learner-centered activity.

Features

Continuous evaluation serves to diagnose weaknesses and permits the teacher to ascertain an individual learner's strengths and weaknesses and her needs. It provides immediate feedback to the teacher, who can then decide whether a particular unit or concept needs a discussion again in the whole class or whether a few individuals are in need of remedial instruction.

By continuous evaluation, children can know their strengths and weaknesses. It provides the child a realistic self assessment of how he/she studies. It can motivate children to develop good study habits, to correct errors, and to direct their activities towards the achievement of desired goals. It helps a learner to determine the areas of instruction in where more emphasis is required.

Continuous evaluation helps in bringing awareness of the achievement to the child, teachers and parents from time to time. They can look into the probable cause of the fall in performance if any, and may take remedial measures of instruction in which more emphasis is required. Many times, because of some personal reasons, family problems or adjustment problems, the children start neglecting their studies, resulting in sudden drop in their performance. If the teacher, child and parents do not notice the sudden drop in the performance of the child in academics, it could result in a permanent deficiency in the childs' learning.

The major emphasis of CCE is on the continuous growth of students ensuring their intellectual, emotional, physical, cultural and social development and therefore, it will not be merely limited to assessment of learner's scholastic attainments. CCE uses assessment as a means of motivating learners to provide feedback and follow up work to improve upon the learning in the classroom and to present a comprehensive picture of a learner's profile.

It is this that has led to the emergence of the concept of School Based Continuous and Comprehensive Evaluation.

SCHOLASTIC AND CO-SCHOLASTIC ASSESSMENT

In order to have Continuous and Comprehensive Evaluation, both Scholastic and Co-Scholastic aspects need to be given due recognition. Such a holistic assessment requires maintaining an ongoing and comprehensive profile for each learner that is honest, encouraging and discreet. While teachers frequently reflect, plan and implement remedial strategies, the child's ability to retain and articulate what has been learned over a period of time also requires periodic assessment. These assessments can take many forms but all of them should be as comprehensive and discreet as possible. *Weekly, fortnightly,* or *quarterly* reviews (depending on the learning area), that do not openly compare one learner with another are generally recommended. The objective is to promote and enhance not just learning and retention among children, but their soft skills as well.

Scholastic Assessment

The objectives of the Scholastic domain are:

- Desirable behaviour related to the learner's knowledge, understanding, application, evaluation, analysis and the ability to apply it in an unfamiliar situation.
- To improve the teaching learning process.
- Assessment should be both *Formative* and *Summative.*

Formative Assessment

Formative Assessment is a tool used by the teacher to continuously monitor student progress in a non-threatening, supportive environment. It involves regular descriptive feedback, a chance for the student to reflect on the performance, take advice and improve upon it. It involves the students' being an essential part of assessment from designing criteria to assessing self or peers. If used effectively, it can improve student performance tremendously while raising the self-esteem of the child and reducing the work load of the teacher.

Formative Assessment is carried out during a course of instruction for providing continuous feedback to both the teachers and the learners. It is also carried out for taking decisions regarding appropriate modifications in the transactional procedures and learning activities.

— often means no more than that the assessment is carried out frequently and is planned at the same time as teaching.

— provides feedback which leads to students recognizing the (learning) gap and closing it. Iit is forward looking.

— includes both feedback and self-monitoring.

— is used essentially to get a feed back into the teaching and learning process.

Features of Formative Assessment

— Is diagnostic and remedial

— Makes provision for effective feedback

— Provides a platform for the active involvement of students in their own learning

— Enables teachers to adjust teaching to take account of the results of assessment

— Recognizes the profound influence assessment has on the motivation and self-esteem of students, both of which are crucial influences on learning

— Recognizes the need for students to be able to assess themselves and understand how to improve

— Builds on students' prior knowledge and experience in designing what is taught

— Incorporates varied learning styles to decide how and what to teach

— Encourages students to understand the criteria that will be used to judge their work

- Offers an opportunity to students to improve their work after they get the feedback
- Helps students to support their peer group and vice-versa.

Summative Assessment

Summative Assessment is carried out at the end of a course of learning. It measures or *'sums-up'* how much a student has learned from the course. It is usually a graded test, i.e., it is marked according to a scale or set of grades. Assessment that is predominantly of summative nature will not by itself be able to yield a valid measure of the growth and development of the student. It, at best, certifies the level of achievement only at a given point of time. The paper-pencil tests are basically a one-time mode of assessment and to exclusively rely on it to decide about the development of a student is not only unfair but also unscientific.

Overemphasis on examination marks that focus on only scholastic aspects in turn makes student assume that assessment is different from learning, resulting in the *'learn and forget'* syndrome. Besides encouraging unhealthy competition, the overemphasis on Summative Assessment system also produces enormous stress and anxiety among the learners.

Features of Summative Assessment

- Assessment *of* learning
- Generally taken by students at the end of a unit or semester to demonstrate the *"sum"* of what they have or have not learned
- Summative assessment methods are the most traditional way of evaluating student work

Table 1. Scholastic Assessment

Formative Assessment (Flexible Timing)		*Summative Assessment (Written, End of Term)*
Tools	*Techniques*	
Questions	Examination	Objective type
Observation schedule	Assignments	Short answer
Interview schedule	Quizzes & competitions	Long answer
Checklist	Projects	
Rating scale	Debates	
Anecdotal records	Elocution	
Document analysis	Group discussions	
Tests and inventories	Club activities	
Portfolio analysis	Experiments	
	Research	

Co-Scholastic Assessment

The desirable behaviour related to learner's life skills, attitudes, interests, values, co-curricular activities and physical health are described as skills to be acquired in co-scholastic domain.

The process of assessing the students' progress in achieving objectives related to scholastic and co-scholastic domain is called comprehensive evaluation. It has been observed that usually under the scholastic domain such as knowledge and understanding of the facts, concepts, principles etc. of a subject are assessed. The Co-Scholastic elements are either altogether excluded from the evaluation process or they are not given adequate attention. For making the evaluation comprehensive, both Scholastic and Co-Scholastic aspects should be given importance. Simple and manageable means of assessment of Co-Scholastic aspects of growth must be included in the comprehensive evaluation scheme.

Comprehensive evaluation would necessitate the use of a variety of tools and techniques. This will be so because both different and specific areas of learner's growth can be evaluated through certain special techniques.

SCHOOL BASED CONTINUOUS AND COMPREHENSIVE EVALUATION

School-based continuous and comprehensive evaluation system should be established to:

- Reduce stress on children
- Make evaluation comprehensive and regular
- Provide space for the teacher for creative teaching
- Provide a tool of diagnosis and remedial action
- Produce learners with greater skills

The aims of School-based CCE are:

- Elimination of chance element and subjectivity, de-emphasis on memorization, encouraging comprehensive evaluation incorporating both scholastic and co-scholastic aspects of learners development
- Continuous evaluation spread over the total span of the instructional time as an integral built-in aspect of the total teaching-learning process
- Functional and meaningful declaration of results for effective use by teachers, students, parents and the society
- Wider uses of test results for purposes not merely of the assessment of levels of pupils' achievements and proficiencies, but mainly for their improvement, thorough diagnosis and remedial/ enrichment programmes
- Improvement in the mechanics of conducting examinations for realizing a number of other allied purposes
- Introduction of concomitant changes in instructional materials and methodology

- Introduction of the semester system
- The use of grades in place of marks in determining and declaring the level of pupil performance and proficiency

The above goals are relevant for both external examination and evaluation in schools.

Characteristics

School Based Evaluation has the following characteristics:

- Is broader, more comprehensive and continuous than traditional system?
- Aims primarily to help learners for systematic learning and development
- Takes care of the needs of the learner as responsible citizens of the future
- Is more transparent, futuristic and provides more scope for associationamong learners, teachers and parents?

School based evaluation provides opportunities to teachers to know the following about their learners:

- What they learn?
- How they learn?
- What type of difficulties/limitations they face in working in tandem?
- What do the children think?
- What do the children feel?
- What are their interests and dispositions?

The focus has shifted to developing a deep learning environment. There is a paradigm shift in the pedagogy and competencies from 'controlling' to 'enriching' to 'empowering' schools.

Traditional Schooling	*Enriching Schooling*	*Empowering Schooling*
Teacher-centred	Student-centred	Experience centred
Subjects and classes—Teacher-directed	Self directed	Virtual authenticity
Sorting and ranking individuals	Continuous assessment	Multi literacies
Competency:	*Competency*:	*Competency*:
Memory	Critical thinking	Risk taking
Competitive	Collaborative	Ethical
	Creative	Interactive

There are Four Assessment Paradigms

1. *Assessment* of *Learning*

The 'assessment of learning' is defined as a process whereby someone attempts to describe and quantify the knowledge, attitudes or skills possessed by another. Teacher direction is paramount and the student has little involvement in the design or implementation of the assessment process in these circumstances.

- Teacher designs learning
- Teacher collects evidence
- Teacher judges what has been learnt

2. *Assessment* for *Learning*

The 'assessment for learning' involves increased level of student autonomy, but not without teacher guidance and collaboration. The assessment for learning is sometimes seen as being akin to 'formative assessment'. There is more emphasis towards giving useful advice to the student and less emphasis on the giving of marks and the grading function.

- Teacher designs learning
- Teacher designs assessment with feedback to student

— Teacher judges what has been learnt.

3. *Assessment* as *Learning*

The 'assessment as learning' is perhaps more connected with diagnostic assessment and can be constructed with more of an emphasis on peer learning. Assessment *as* learning generates opportunities for self assessment and peer assessment. Students take on increased responsibility to generate quality information about their learning and that of others.

- Teacher and student co-construct learning
- Teacher and student co-construct assessment
- Teacher and student co-construct learning progress map

Assessment for learning and assessment as learning activities should be deeply embedded in teaching and learning and be the source of interactive feedback, allowing students to adjust, re-think and re-learn.

4. *Assessment in Learning*

The 'assessment in learning' places the question at the centre of teaching and learning. It deflects the teaching from its focus on a 'correct answer' to a focus on 'a fertile question'. Through enquiry students engage in processes that generates feedback about their learning, which come from multiple sources and activities. It contributes to the construction of other learning activities, line of enquiry and the generation of other questions.

- Student as the centre of learning
- Student monitors, assesses and reflects on learning
- Student initiates demonstration of learning (to self and others)
- Teacher as coach and mentor

Teachers and students need to understand the purpose of each assessment strategy. The overall assessment 'package' being used by learners and teachers should accurately capture, generate and use meaningful learning information to generate deep learning and understanding.

CCE IN MIDDLE SCHOOL LEVEL

The Central Board of Secondary Education (CBSE) has introduced the scheme of Continuous and Comprehensive Evaluation in its schools in a phased manner. In 2004, CCE was implemented in primary classes at I-V. Besides doing away with the concept of pass/ fail system upto class V, the assessment focused on the positive aspects of the child's development during this stage. Accordingly Achievement Records for the primary classes (for Classes I and II and Classes III to V) were also developed and recommended to schools with the objective of facilitating holistic learning. As a follow up, the Board decided to extend CCE to classes VI to VIII in 2006.

In the year 2000, the Board implemented the concept of an independent Certificate of School Based Evaluation to be awarded by the school to all students who passed CBSE Class X Examination. This certificate was awarded in addition to the Board's regular certificate and marks statement related to external examination. It carried a footnote that a certificate of CCE is being issued by the school and should be studied for judging the total personality of the student. Besides scholastic areas, co-scholastic areas were included in CCE for assessment over a continuous period of two years i.e. Classes IX and X.

Details of CCE Report Book for Classes VI, VII and VIII

Part 1 consists of the evaluation of Scholastic Areas.

Part 1: Scholastic Areas

- There will be two terms. The First Term will be from April-September and the Second Term from October-March of the subsequent year.
- Each term will have two Formative and one Summative Assessment.
- Assessment will be indicated in Grades.
- The Grading Scale for the Scholastic Areas is a Nine Point Grading Scale.
- Overall grade of Formative Assessments over the two terms (FA1+FA2+FA3+FA4) and the overall grade of Summative Assessment (SA1+SA2) must be given. The total of the two grades which comprises (Formative and Summative) needs to be given in the relevant column.

Part-2: Co-Scholastic Areas

Part 2 consists of Co-Scholastic Areas where students' are assessed in four parts on a Five Point Grading Scale once in a session

Part 2(A):

Life Skills consists of:

- Self Awareness
- Problem Solving
- Decision Making Critical Thinking
- Creative Thinking
- Interpersonal Relationships
- Effective Communication
- Empathy
- Managing Emotions

— Dealing with Stress

Part 2(B):

— Work Education

Part 2(C):

— Visual and Performing Arts

Part 2(D): Attitudes & Values

— Attitudes towards Teachers, Schoolmates, School Programmes and Environment.

— Value systems refers to the framework which must be developed right through Primary to Secondary level.

These are to be filled in after a period of observation over the year by the Class Teacher in consultation with the subject teachers.

Part 3: Co-Curricular Activities

Part 3 consists of Co-curricular Activities wherein choice in participation and assessment thereof is available. It has two sub parts to be assessed on a five-point grading scale.

Part 3(A)

1. Literary and Creative Skills
2. Scientific Skills
3. Information and Communication Technology (ICT)
4. Organizational and Leadership Skills (Clubs)

A student will be expected to choose two activities from these four groups and will be assessed on their level of participation and achievement.

Part 3(B) Health and Physical Activities

Eight different kinds of Health and Physical Activities have been provided.

1. Sports/ Indigenous sports (Kho-Kho etc.)
2. NCC/NSS
3. Scouting and Guiding
4. Swimming
5. Gymnastics
6. Yoga
7. First Aid
8. Gardening/*Shramdaan*

Students will be assessed on any two activities that are chosen from within the eight different activities. The objective is to benefit from Physical activities to maximize health benefits. They will be assessed by teachers involved in various activities in school.

The areas given in the Report Book provide adequate opportunities to the learners for all round development. It has been widely understood that class room transaction in academic subjects alone cannot foster development in all areas or help to develop Life Skills. The development of qualities such as Self-Esteem, Positive Attitude and Life Skills require development of positive and adaptive behaviors over a period of time. These Life Skills can be integrated into the entire personality of a learner over the ten years of schooling and are essential for fostering personal qualities, nurturing good relationships and developing effective Communication Skills. The development of good physical health, formation of positive attitude towards others including environment and cultivation of universal values is possible only through learner's involvement in Life Skills and Co-Curricular Activities.

Evaluation of Scholastic Aspect

Part 1: Scholastic Areas

Evaluation of Academic Subjects in Classes VI to VIII.

Six assessments are proposed:

Type of assessment	*Percentage of weighting in academic session*	*Month*	*Term wise weighting*
	First Term		
Formative Assessment-1	10%	April-May	FA1+FA2=20%
Formative Assessment-2	10%	July-August	
Summative Assessment-1	30%	September	SA1=30%
	Second Term		
Formative Assessment-3	10%	October-November	FA3+FA4=20%
Formative Assessment-4	10%	January-February	
Summative Assessment-2	30%	March	SA2=30%

Total:

Formative Assessments (FA) = FA1+FA2+ FA3+FA4 = 40%
Summative Assessments (SA) = SA1+SA2 = 60%

All across the schools, the most commonly used tools/ techniques are those developed by teachers themselves. Among these are paper-pencil tests/tasks, written and oral tests, questions on pictures, simulated activities and discussion with students. Short class tests are used by most teachers as a quick and easy way of assessing the learning progress of children. As these are generally conducted at the end of a unit/month covering the specified content taught during that period, these are no doubt useful but they need to be used effectively.

Similarly, tests can be formal, informal, written or oral, based on specified content desired to be tested. They are diagnostic in nature as they enable the teacher to identify or reveal the strength and weaknesses of students. A test should not create any fear among students and it should be administered in an informal way.

Grading Scale

Assessment of Scholastic attainments Part 1 will be reported twice in a year. The nine point grading scale for measuring Scholastic achievements is given below:

Grade	*Marks Range*	*Grade point*
A1	91-100	10.0
A2	81-90	9.0
B1	71-80	8.0
B2	61-70	7.0
C1	51-60	6.0
C2	41-50	5.0
D	33-40	4.0
E1	21-32	3.0
E2	00-20	2.0

Minimum qualifying grade in all the subjects under Scholastic Domain is D.

All assessment with regard to the academic status of the students shall be done in marks and the assessment will be given in grades. Co-Scholastic attainments 2(A,B,C and D) and 3(A,B) will be done on 5 point Scale (shown in the table below). It will be done once in a session.

Grade	*Grade Points*
A	4.1-5.0
B	3.1-4.0
C	2.1-3.0
D	1.1-2.0
E	0-1.0

Minimum qualifying grade in Co-Scholastic Domain is D.

As per the Directives of RTE, no child will be detained till class VIII

Format of Report Book for Classes VI to VIII

The suggested format of a Report Book is given below.

School
Logo

Affiliation No..
Name of School..
Complete Address..
E-mail ID..
Telephone No..

Report Book
CLASSES VI to VIII
Session:..........................

Student Profile:
Name of Student...
Class/House..
Admission No..
Date of Birth..
Mother's name..
Father's name...
Residential Address
and Telephone No...

Attendance:	Term I	Term II
Total attendance of the student	....	....
Total working days	....	....

Signature: *Student* *Class Teacher* *Principal* *Parent*

Part-I: Academic Performance: Scholastic Areas(9 point scale)

S.No	*Subjects*	*Term-I*				*Term-II*				*(Term I+II)*		
		FA1	*FA2*	*SA1*	*FA1+ FA2+ SA1*	*FA3*	*FA4*	*SA2*	*FA3+ FA4+ SA2*	*FA1+FA2+ FA3+FA4*	*SA1+ SA2*	*Over-all grade*
01	Language I											
02	Language II											
03	Language III											
04	Mathematics											
05	Science											
06	Social Science											
07	Addl. Subject											

Overall Grade ____________

Part 2: Co-Scholastic Areas
(to be assessed on a 5 point scale once in a session)

2 (A): Life Skills

S.No.	*Descriptive Indicators**	*Grade*
01	Self-Awareness:	
02	Problem Solving:	
03	Decision-Making:	
04	Critical Thinking:	
05	Creative Thinking:	
06	Interpersonal Relationships:	
07	Effective Communication:	
08	Empathy:	
09	Managing Emotions:	
10	Dealing with Stress:	

* Descriptive Indicators are statements used to describe each learner—

2(B): Work Education

Descriptive Indicators	Grade

2(C): Visual and Performing Arts

Descriptive Indicators	Grade

Suggestive Activities:

Work Education: Cookery Skills, Preparation of stationery items, Tieing and dyeing and screen printing, preparing paper out of waste paper, Hand embroidery, Running a book bank, Repair and maintenance of domestic electrical gadgets, Computer operation and maintenance, Photography etc.

Visual & Performing Arts: Music (Vocal, Instrumental), Dance, Drama, Drawing, Painting, Craft, Sculpture, Puppetry, Folk Art forms etc.

2(D): Attitudes & Values

S.No.	*Descriptive Indicators*	*Grade*
0.1	Attitude Towards:	
01.1	Teachers:	
01.2	School-mates:	
01.3	School Programme and Environment:	
0.2	Value Systems:	

3(A) *Co-Scholastic Activities (Any two to be assessed)*

1. Literary and Creative Skills; 2. Scientific Skills; 3. Information and Communication Technology (ICT); 4. Organizational and Leadership Skills (Clubs)

S.No.	*Descriptive Indicators*	*Grade*
01		
02		

Suggestive Activities:

Literary & Creative Skills: Debate, Declamation, Creative Writing, Recitation, Poster-Making, Slogan Writing, Theatre etc.

Scientific Skills: Science Club, Projects, Maths Club, Science Quiz, Science Exhibition, Olympiads etc.

Information and Communication Technology (ICT): PowerPoint Presentation, Website and Cover Page Designing, Animation, Programming, E-books etc.

Organizational & Leadership Skills : Eco Club, Health & Wellness Club, Heritage Club, Disaster Management Club, Literary Club, Scientific Club and other Clubs etc.

3(B) Health and Physical Education (Any two to be assessed)

1. Sports/Indigenous Sports 2. NCC/NSS 3. Scouting and Guiding 4. Swimming 5. Gymnastics 6. Yoga 7. First Aid 8. Gardening/*Shramdaan*

S.No.	*Descriptive Indicators*	*Grade*
01		
02		

Self-Awareness

My Goals:

Strengths:

My Interests and Hobbies:

Responsibilities Discharged /Exceptional Achievements:

Health Status

Height................................ Weight...
Blood Group........................Vision (L)............... (R).................
Dental Hygiene...

Scholastic Areas (Grading on 9 point scale)		
Grade	*Marks Range*	*Grade Point*
A1	91-100	10.0
A2	81-90	9.0
B1	71-80	8.0
B2	61-70	7.0
C1	51-60	6.0
C2	41-50	5.0
D	33-40	4.0
E1	21-32	3.0
E2	00-20	2.0

Co-Scholastic Areas (Grading on 5 point scale)

Grade	*Grade Points*
A	4.1-5.0
B	3.1-4.0
C	2.1-3.0
D	1.1-2.0
E	0-1.0

Student must obtain the qualifying grade (minimum grade D) in all the subjects under Scholastic and Co-Scholastic Domain.

Proposed Evaluation Scheme for Scholastic Subjects

In order to help students improve their performance levels, the schools shall diagnose their learning difficulties through formative tests right from the beginning of the academic year and bring it to the notice of parents at appropriate intervals of time. They will recommend suitable remedial steps to enhance their learning capability. Similarly especially gifted children should be provided with further reinforcements by giving them additional assignments, enrichment material and mentoring. Due provision should be made in the class timetable for mentoring and to address different kinds of learners. The teacher also needs to incorporate strategies for dealing with differently abled students in her class.

The Formative assessment should normally be made on recorded evidences based on anecdotal records to be maintained by the class teacher or the subject teacher.

It will be advisable to communicate levels of attainment to the students and parents during the course of the academic year, so that with their cooperation the remedial measures are taken in time for enhancing the performance of the students. The overall assessment should be followed by the descriptive remarks by the class teacher about the positive and significant achievements, avoiding negative assessment even by implication. It implies:

- Sharing learning goals with students. Involving students in self-assessment
- Providing feedback which leads to students recognising and taking next steps
- Being confident that, every student can improve

Specific Recommendations for Formative Assessment

Listed below are a few recommendations for Formative Assessment which can be followed by schools. This list gives suggestions month-wise for various subjects. It is advised that within each term, schools use the paper-pencil test only once for assessing student performance under Formative Assessment. The purpose is to ensure use of multiple modules of assessment so that the focus on written tests is reduced.

In order to fulfil the objectives of Formative Assessment and to enable students to improve performance, teachers need to use a variety of assessment tools during the course of their teaching. It is mandatory that teachers use at least 3-4 different assessment tools during the term for each Formative Assessment (FA). This list given below is not exhaustive, it is only to give an idea of the variety possible.

Formative Assessment can be carried through using multiple modes of assessment such as assignments, quizzes, debates, group discussions, projects. It may be clearly communicated to all teachers teaching various subjects that all projects and assignments must be done as group activities, within the class and school time only. Each subject must have only one paper-pencil test under Formative Assessment. The other modes of Assessment must be a part of classroom interactive activities.

Languages

- *Oral and listening*—these could be listening comprehension,prepared speech, conversation or dialogue
- *Written assignments*—short/long question answers, creative writing, reports, newspaper articles, diary entries, poetry etc.
- *Speeches*—debates, oratory, recitation, extempore etc.
- *Research projects*—information gathering, deductive reasoning, analysis and synthesis and a presentation using a variety of forms including the use of Information Technology (IT)
- Pair work/group work
- Peer assessment

It is suggested in Languages at least some assessment should be for assessing Conversation Skills.

Mathematics

- Problem solving, Multiple choice questions (MCQ)
- Data handling and analysis
- Investigative projects
- Math Lab activities
- Models including origami etc.
- Research projects and presentations
- Group projects
- Peer assessment
- Presentations including the use of Information Technology (IT)

It is suggested for Mathematics at least some formative assessment tasks should be based on Maths Lab Activities.

Sciences

- Written assignments, MCQ
- Experimental work which may involve one or more of setting experiments, making observations, handling data, making deductions, working safely
- Planning or designing experiments to collect data or to investigate properties, laws, phenomena etc.
- Research work which could be investigative or information gathering and deducing
- Group work—research or experimental
- Contextual research projects
- Peer assessment
- Presentations including the use of Information Technology (IT)
- Science Quiz
- Seminar
- Symposium
- Field Tour
- Class Response
- Model Making

It is suggested that for Science at least some formative assessments in the year are Experiments and hands-on activities.

Socia Sciences

- *Written assignments*—short and long answers
- Commentaries
- Source-based analysis
- *Projects*—investigative, informative, deductive and analytical

- Research
- *Group work*—projects and presentations
- Models and charts
- Presentations, including the use of Information Technology (IT)
- Using authentic sources and primary texts
- Open book tests
- Secondary sources
- Comparison and contrast

It is suggested in Social Science that at least some assessment should be based on projects which are done in groups as in-class activities under the direct supervision of the teacher.

ASSESSING CO-SCHOLASTIC AREAS

Collecting Evidence and Interpreting

Learning in Scholastic and Co-Scholastic Areas is demonstrated by change of behaviour in the learner. Behaviour is of two kinds—covert and overt. Overt behaviour is the outer expression of covert behaviour. As a teacher, you can judge a student only by his/ her overt behaviour. For example, understanding is covert; you really do not know whether a student has understood even if he/she says "Yes, Ma'am". However, when the student explains to you the concept, you know for sure his/her level of understanding. In this example, 'explain' is the overt behaviour and 'understand' is the covert behaviour.

Overt behaviour of a student provides us evidence to assess his/her level of learning. Evaluation is all about collecting evidence and interpreting the human behaviour based on the evidence. Unlike robots or programmed instruments, human beings have a mind and are flexible. Hence, we prefer repeated evidence and then see the trend. For example, a student may be sometimes joyful, some times sad and yet on some other occasions angry. You may not be able to draw a conclusion—whether the student is joyful or not. But, if a student is courteous to you most of the time, and courteous to all your colleague teachers most of the time, you can safely conclude, 'the student is very courteous'. Isn't it?

Thus, assessment of human behaviour is collecting repeated evidences (information), identifying the trend of behaviour, deriving conclusions or making judgements and providing feedback. Since, we the assessors are also human beings, and are subject to our own beliefs, values, moods and emotions, we can 'be' and often 'are' subjective in interpretation. For example, a student expresses his/her difference of opinion to a stated view/ position with respect to a concept or a practice in the class. A 'classical' teacher will construe it as indiscipline and ask her to behave, whereas a 'neo-modern' teacher will construe it as divergence and enter into a discourse with an open mind. The latter will rate the same behaviour as very positive and creative. Research on human behaviour recommends use of 'triangulation' technique—collecting and interpreting evidence by multiple assessors (at least three in number).

To sum up, it may include the following steps:

- Identifying qualities
- Specifying behaviours/indicators of the concerned area/skill
- Collection of evidence in respect of behaviour/ indicators through observation and other techniques

– Recording of the evidences
– Analysis of the recorded evidences
– Reporting or awarding grades

The analysis of records raised as a result of periodic observation is done to validate the attainment of the quality resulting in growth in the Co-Scholastic Areas. The grades and descriptive indicators are assigned on the basis of the degree of attainment of a particular skill/ behavior outcome.

We have so far used a few terminologies that are landmarks in human behaviour assessment. These are:

1. Overt behaviour
2. Evidence of behaviour
3. Trend of behaviour
4. Triangulation

Thus, our fundamental challenge in assessing students in Co-Scholastic Areas are four-fold:

a. Identifying (overt) behavioural indicators for each of the chosen areas
b. Creating a scheme of assessment for certification
c. Tools and techniques of gathering data and evidence
d. Data archiving, interpreting and certifying

Overt Behaviour Indicators

Just to remind you, we have chosen the following Co-Scholastic Areas. These are:

1. Life Skills
2. Work Education
3. Visual and Performing Arts

4. Attitudes and Values
5. Literary and Creative Skills
6. Scientific Skills
7. Information and Communication Technology (ICT)
8. Organization and Leadership Skills (Clubs)
9. Health and Physical Education:
   9.1 Sports/Indigenous Sports
   9.2 NCC/NSS
   9.3 Scouting and Guiding
   9.4 Swimming
   9.5 Gymnastics
   9.6 Yoga
   9.7 First Aid
   9.8 Gardening/*Shramdaan*

Life Skills

Life Skills are abilities for adaptive and positive behaviour that enable individuals to deal effectively with the demands and challenges of everyday life. They are abilities that facilitate the physical, mental and emotional well-being of individuals.

'Adaptive' means that a person is flexible in approach and able to adjust to different circumstances.

'Positive behaviour' implies that a person is forward looking and finds a ray of hope, solution and opportunities even in difficult situations.

Life Skills are abilities that will help students to be successful in living a productive life. Learning and practising Life Skills help students to improve their personal and social qualities.

There are large number of Life Skills emanating from various sources. For practical purposes and for feasibility, we have chosen ten Life Skills as given in the table below:

Life Skills Matrix

Sl.No.	*Life Skills*
1.	Self-awareness
2.	Problem Solving
3.	Decision-Making
4.	Critical Thinking
5.	Creative Thinking
6.	Interpersonal Relationships
7.	Effective Communication
8.	Empathy
9.	Managing Feelings/Emotions
10.	Dealing with Stress

Although all or most of the Life Skills can be measured by standardized tests and inventories, such skills can also be reasonably assessed on the basis of displayed behaviour by the student. We have provided a few sampled observable behaviours.

As mentioned earlier, students will be assessed in these domains on the basis of their overt behaviour. We will take three different courses of action to build in objectivity and reliability:

— Day-to-day observation

— Rating per term

— Testing annually

Day to day observation

Please keep 'a watchful eye' on your student, whenever you notice a significant behaviour that may shed light on any one of the fifty (50) descriptors under the 10 domains. Record it in your diary. It should not be time bound; it should be as and when such a thing happens. Here are a few examples:

- Rohan shared his tiffin with his friends today.
- Jiten gulped his tiffin quickly and then looked at others.
- Though Sara did not figure in the list of awardees, she was all smiles and helped me in organizing the event.
- George visited his sick classmate at home and briefed him about the home work.
- Sarbari differed with my viewpoint; she argued but never got irritated; but Shanti got angry because Sarbari was arguing with me.
- Mohammad connected the computer to the LCD projector, set the screen so proficiently that could use it in the classroom.

While you rate such behaviour, please remember '5' stands for desirable behaviour and less than '1' for the undesirable ones. For example in the above case Sarbari gets '5', but Shanti gets '2' or '1'. Although you would observe on a day to day basis and record, you would only accumulate it at the end of the term and then convert into a grade.

All these statements reveal certain styles of behaviour of a student, e.g. effective communication of Sarbari, excellent interpersonal skills exhibited by Mohammad and Sara's ability to manage her emotions, etc.

Rating at the end of the term

In the following pages, we present you behaviour descriptors for each of the Co-Scholastic dimensions. Human behaviour, as you know, is not a binary function; does not appear in 'yes' or 'no'. It differs in degrees. Hence, rate each behaviour on five-point scale once in a session:

Grade	*Grade Points*
A	4.1-5.0
B	3.1-4.0
C	2.1-3.0
D	1.1-2.0
E	0-1.0

How to Calculate Grades in Co-Scholastic Areas?

1. Each student will be graded on each of the 10 Life Skills, Work Education, Visual and Performing Arts, 03 Attitudes, Values, 02 Co-curricular Activities and 02 Health and Physical Education (HPE) Activities.
2. Maximum score for each Life Skill is 25, for Work Education, Visual and Performing Arts and Attitudes is 50, for Values is 200 and for Co-curricular Activities and HPE is 50.
3. Before assigning the Grades on each component using the conversion table, please calculate the average or grade points by dividing the total score obtained by a student by number of items in that component. For example, for a student who has a score of 15 in Self-awareness; you need to divide it by the number of descriptors, i.e. 5; the average or grade point is 3.0; hence grade is C.
4. A Sample Sheet to calculate grades in Co-Scholastic Areas is given after the discussion of the indicators.

(i) Self Awareness

Sl.No.	Descriptors	Score out of 5
1.	Is aware of his/her physical/social and emotional self?	
2.	Self-respecting	
3.	Aware of his/her strengths and weaknesses	
4.	Adopts optimistic approach	
5.	Has the confidence to face challenges?	
Total		
Average/Grade		

(ii) Problem Solving

Sl.No.	*Descriptors*	*Score out of 5*
1.	Finds a workable solution to the problem	
2.	Handles various problems effectively	
3.	Identifies and states the problem	
4.	Views problems as a stepping stone to success	
5.	Finds ways to solve different kinds of conflicts	
Total		
Average/Grade		

(iii) Decision Making

Sl.No.	*Descriptors*	*Score out of 5*
1.	Is decisive and convincing?	
2.	Is able to find different alternatives to solve problems?	
3.	Is able to analyse the alternatives critically?	
4.	Takes decisions logically	
5.	Shows readiness to face challenges	
Total		
Average/Grade		

(iv) Critical Thinking

Sl.No.	*Descriptors*	*Score out of 5*
1.	Assesses the statements and arguments	
2.	Examines the problems closely	
3.	Listens carefully and gives feedback	
4.	Tries to find out alternatives and solutions	
5.	Questions relevantly	
Total		
Average/Grade		

(v) Creative Thinking

Sl.No.	*Descriptors*	*Score out of 5*
1.	Ability to find creative and constructive solutions to problems and issues	
2	Is independent in thinking?	
3.	Has fluency in expression?	
4.	Has rich imagination and is able to think out of the box?	
5.	Can make independent judgement in crucial matters?	
Total		
Average/Grade		

(vi) Interpersonal Relationships

Sl.No.	*Descriptors*	*Score out of 5*
1.	Is able to interact effectively with peers and teachers?	
2.	Is very cheerful and friendly?	
3.	Exhibits fine etiquettes and other social skills	
4.	Finds it natural and easy to share and discuss the feelings with others	
5.	Responsive to others' interests & concerns	
Total		
Average/Grade		

(vii) Effective Communication

Sl.No.	Descriptors	Score out of 5
1.	Contributes frequently to group conversations	
2.	Knows the difference between assertive, aggressive and submissive manners of communication	
3.	Is able to make use of speech, action and expression while communicating?	
4.	Exhibits good listening skills	
5.	Uses gestures, facial expressions and voice intonation to emphasize points	
Total		
Average/Grade		

(viii) Empathy

Sl.No.	Descriptors	Score out of 5
1.	Demonstrates ability to respect others	
2.	Is concerned about the problems in the society/community	
3.	Is able to reach out to the friends who are in need of extra help?	
4.	Is tolerant with diversity?	
5.	Is sensitive towards the environment?	
Total		
Average/Grade		

(ix) Managing Emotions

Sl.No.	Descriptors	Score out of 5
1.	Is able to identify his/her emotions?	
2.	Manages his/her emotions	
3.	Shares his/her feelings with peer group, teachers and parents	
4.	Can express his/her feelings in a healthy manner?	
5.	Remains cool and calm under adverse conditions	
Total		
Average/Grade		

(x) Dealing with Stress

Sl.No.	*Descriptors*	*Score out of 5*
1.	Is able to identify the different stress related situations?	
2.	Copes with stress in an effective manner	
3.	Is optimistic in handling different stress inducing situations?	
4.	Able to react positively under critical situations	
5.	Remains composed and collected in stressful situations	
Total		
Average/Grade		

Work Education

Sl.No.	*Descriptors*	*Score out of 5*
1.	Has a collaborative approach towards the process of learning?	
2.	Is Innovative in ideas?	
3.	Plans and adheres to timelines	
4.	Is Involved and motivated?	
5.	Demonstrates a positive attitude	
6.	Is helpful, guides and facilitates others?	
7.	Demonstrates an understanding of correlation with real life situations	
8.	Has a step-by-step approach to solving a problem?	
9.	Has clear understanding of output to be generated?	
10.	Is able to apply the theoretical knowledge into practical usage?	
Total		
Average/Grade		

Visual and Performing Arts

(i) Visual Arts

Sl.No.	Descriptors	Score out of 5
1.	Takes an innovative and creative approach	
2.	Shows aesthetic sensibilities	
3.	Displays observation skills	
4.	Demonstrates interpretation and originality	
5.	Corelates with real life	
6.	Shows willingness to experiment with different art modes and mediums	
7.	Sketches or paints	
8.	Generates computer animation	
9.	Demonstrates proportion in size and clarity	
10.	Understands the importance of colour, balance and brightness	
Total		
Average/Grade		

(ii) Performing Arts

Sl.No.	Descriptors	Score out of 5
1.	Sings and plays instrumental music	
2.	Dances and acts in drama	
3.	Awareness and appreciation of works of artists	
4.	Demonstrates appreciation skills	
5.	Participates actively in aesthetic activities at various levels	
6.	Takes initiative to plan, create and direct various creative events	
7.	Reads and shows a degree of awareness of particular domain of art	
8.	Experiments with art forms	
9.	Shows a high degree of imagination and innovation	
10.	Displays artistic temperament in all of his/her actions in school and outside	
Total		
Average/Grade		

Attitudes

Attitude is an important dimension in students' lives. In this section, you will assess students' attitude with respect to the teachers, school-mates, and school programmes. Please follow the same practice as in the assessment of Life Skills.

(i) Attitudes towards Teachers

Sl.No.	*Descriptors*	*Score out of 5*
1.	Shows decency and courtesy to teachers inside and outside the class	
2.	Demonstrates positive attitudes towards learning	
3.	Takes suggestions and criticism in the right spirit	
4.	Respects teachers' instructions	
5.	Accepts norms and rules of the school	
6.	Communicates his/her thoughts with teachers	
7.	Confides his/her problems with teachers	
8.	Shows honesty and sincerity towards teachers	
9.	Feels free to ask questions	
10.	Helpful to teachers	
Total		
Average/Grade		

(ii) Attitude towards School-mates

Sl.No.	*Descriptors*	*Score out of 5*
1.	Is friendly with most of the classmates?	
2.	Expresses ideas and opinions freely in a group	
3.	Is receptive to ideas and opinion of others?	
4.	Treats classmates as equals (without any sense of superiority or inferiority)	

5.	Sensitive and supportive towards peers and differently abled schoolmates	
6.	Treats peers from different social, religious and economic background without any discrimination	
7.	Respects opposite gender and is comfortable in their company	
8.	Does not bully others	
9.	Deals with aggressive behaviour (bullying) by peers tactfully	
10.	Shares credit and praise with team members and peers	
Total		
Average/Grade		

(iii) Attitude towards School Programmes and Environment

Sl.No.	*Descriptors*	*Score out of 5*
1.	Attaches a lot of importance to school activities and programmes	
2.	Participates in school activities relating to improvement of environment	
3.	Enthusiastically participates in school programmes	
4.	Shoulders responsibility happily	
5.	Confronts any one who criticizes school and school programmes	
6.	Insists on parents to participate/witness school programmes	
7.	Participates in community activities relating to environment	
8.	Takes care of school property	
9.	Sensitive and concerned about environmental degradation	
10.	Takes initiative in planning activities for the betterment of the environment	
Total		
Average/Grade		

Value Systems

Values are determining qualities of life. There is a very large body of knowledge and lists of values. Article 51A of the Indian Constitution—Fundamental Duties—provides the most comprehensive list of values that should be inculcated in every Indian citizen. There are 10 principles; we have identified four behavioural descriptors for each—in all 40 descriptors. Like the previous ones, please assign a score out of 5 and calculate the average across the 40 behavioural descriptors and assign the grades as per the scheme mentioned earlier.

(i) To abide by the constitution and respect its ideals and institutions, the National Flag annd the National Anthem

	Descriptors	*Score out of 5*
a.	Is aware of the Directive Principle and Fundamental Rights enshrined in the Constitution?	
b.	Sings National Anthem and patriotic songs with decorum	
c.	Attends hoisting of National Flag with respect and decorum	
d.	Understands the meaning of tri colour and the Ashok Chakra	

(ii) To cherish and follow the noble ideals which inspired freedom struggle

	Descriptors	*Score out of 5*
a.	Takes interest in the National Freedom Struggle	
b.	Displays pride in being an Indian citizen	
c.	Participates in celebration of Republic Day and Independence Day with enthusiasm	
d.	Reads biographies of freedom fighters	

(iii) To uphold and protect the sovereignty, unity and integrity of India

	Descriptors	*Score out of 5*
a.	Stays alert and raises voice against divisive forces	
b.	Respects armed forces and paramilitary forces	
c.	Respects Indian diversity	
d.	Maintains peace and love	

(iv) To defend the country and render national service when called upon to do so

	Descriptors	*Score out of 5*
a.	Shows a proactive and responsible behaviour during crises	
b.	Helpful towards disadvantaged section of the society	
c.	Renders social work enthusiastically	
d.	Actively participates in community development programmes of the school	

(v) To promote harmony and spirit of unity and brotherhood amongst all the people of India transcending religious, linguistic and regional or sectional diversities; to remove the practices derogatory to the dignity of women

	Descriptors	*Score out of 5*
a.	Respects opposite gender	
b.	Respects teachers from different religious and linguistic communities	
c.	Takes up issues in case of indignity to women	
d.	Kind and helpful towards classmates and people of community	

(vi) To value and preserve the rich heritage of our culture.

	Descriptors	*Score out of 5*
a.	Reads and discusses about the Indian culture and heritage	
b.	Appreciates diversity of cultures, social practices and more	
c.	Treasures the belongings of the school, community and the country with a sense of pride	
d.	Protects and prevents defacing of national monuments	

(vii) To protect and improve natural environment

	Descriptors	*Score out of 5*
a.	Shows compassion for living creatures	
b.	Takes active interest in maintaining flora, fauna, plants and gardens	
c.	Participates in movements for protecting endangered animals and green cover	
d.	Takes care to clean classroom, school and neighbourhood	

(viii) To develop scientific temper and the spirit of enquiry

	Descriptors	*Score out of 5*
a.	Experiments to find new solutions	
b.	Analyzes and critically evaluates events on the basis of data and information	
c.	Questions and verifies knowledge	
d.	Explains processes and products logically	

(ix) To safeguard public property and to abjure violence

	Descriptors	*Score out of 5*
a.	Takes care of school furniture and property	
b.	Resists defacing and decimation of public property	

c.	Does not fight and harm others	
d.	Does not affiliate to groups and communities who believe and promote violence	

(x) To strive towards excellence in all spheres of individual and collective activity which leads to higher level of performance

	Descriptors	*Score out of 5*
a.	Makes an effort to improve academic performance in school	
b.	Makes special efforts to improve on Co-Scholastic areas	
c.	Strives to identify potential and actualize with effort	
d.	Aspires and strives for excellence in education and life	

Total Score

Average Score/Grade

Co-Curricular Activities

(i) Literary and Creative Skills

Sl.No.	*Descriptors*	*Score out of 5*
1.	Composes poems or lyrics	
2.	Writes short stories	
3.	Writes literary criticism	
4.	Participates actively in literary and creative activities at school, inter school, state, national and international levels	
5.	Plans and organizes literary events like debates, recitation, book clubs etc.	
6.	Reads books and shows a high degree of awareness in the field of literature	
7.	Appreciates well written or spoken pieces representing various genres (prose, poetry, plays)	

8.	Expresses ideas and opinions creatively in different forms	
9.	Displays originality of ideas and opinions	
10.	Is able to inspire others and involve a large part of the school and community in different events?	

Total

Average/Grade

(ii) Scientific Skills

Sl.No.	*Descriptors*	*Score out of 5*
1.	Verifies existing knowledge before accepting	
2.	Does not get carried away by rumours and media reports?	
3.	Tries to find new and more effective solutions to problems	
4.	Conducts experiments with efficiency and effectiveness	
5.	Takes keen interest in scientific activities in laboratory and field-based experiment at school, inter-school, state, national and international level	
6.	Takes the initiative to plan, organize and evaluate various science-related events like quizzes, seminars, model making etc.	
7.	Shows a high degree of curiosity and reads science-related literature	
8.	Is a keen observer and is able to take decisions?	
9.	Displays good experimental skills and a practical knowledge of every day phenomena	
10.	Making use of technology in making projects and models)	

Total

Average/Grade

(iii) Information and Communication Technology (ICT)

Sl.No.	Descriptors	Score out of 5
1.	Is efficient in handling IT equipments and gadgets?	
2.	Has a step by step approach to solving a problem?	
3.	Is able to apply theoretical knowledge into practical usage?	
4.	Plants and adheres to activity and project time lines	
5.	Takes initiative in organizing and participating in technology related events e.g IT fairs, competitions etc.	
6.	Takes keen interest in computer related activities	
7.	Is helpful, guides and facilitates others?	
8.	Is a keen observer and is able to make decisions?	
9.	Is innovative in ideas?	
10.	Adheres to ethical norms of using technology?	

Total

Average/Grade

(iv) Organizational and Leadership SkillsPlease record the Club in which the student is participating.

Sl.No.	Descriptors	Score out of 5
1.	Helps and organizes events in that capacity	
2.	Demonstrates ability to work in teams	
3.	Can organize work groups in short time?	
4.	Actively participates in School Clubs, e.g. Science, Eco-Clubs, Health and Wellness Clubs, Heritage Clubs and other clubs—	
5.	Represents class, school, inter-school and at various other levels	
6.	Takes initiative to plan and manage different kinds of events like festivals, environment week, fund raisers,	

(Contd...)

	seminars, quizzes, arranging morning assembly etc.	
7.	Exhibits collaboration and co-ordination skills while executing the tasks	
8.	Displays originality of ideas and the ability to see them through	
9.	Delivers assigned jobs with responsibility	
10.	Is a keen observer and is able to take decisions?	
Total		
Average/Grade		

Health and Physical Education

Proper development of the body is essential for the healthy growth of the mind. It is therefore, necessary that the students should be examined by qualified doctors once in the session along with a follow-up session. If this facility is not available general information about health i.e. height and weight, etc. could be obtained by the teacher. There are already age/ sex related charts of height and weight, and teachers should use these charts and note observations on the basis of entries she/he makes in the Report Book.

In addition to this general information, physical disabilities and diseases e.g. defective vision, maintenance of teeth, deafness, long absence due to illness, which the teacher can detect at one's own level, should also be noted. He/she should also bring any noticeable handicap to the notice of the parents. In the assessment of Health Status, the recordings of height shall be in centimeters and the weight shall be mentioned in kilograms. The Helath Manuals (in four volumes) brought out by CBSE must be referred to and the graded activities taken up as part of the curriculum in school. Moreover features of Health Promoting Schools, format of Health Cards and the themes and Annexures must be adhered to. The suggested format of Health Cards has also been given in the Comprehensive School Health Manual (Volume I). The Health Card records the history in terms of health for all learners from the time of admission to the school till they leave.

While the area of Physical Education of the curriculum will be judging the skills and proficiencies acquired by the students in games, sports, physical education etc, the area of Health Education will concentrate on those aspects which constitute the criteria for determining the physical health of an individual. The following aspects will be taken care of in this area.

Health Education needs to be assessed on the basis of:

- Basic understanding about health
- Physical fitness
- Attitude development
- Participation in Health and Wellness Club activities

The teacher's responsibility in this area will be limited to general observations for being communicated to the parents and guardians on the above aspects of health of all students.

We divided this domain into two segments. One is rating certain Health and Physical Education (HPE) related behaviours, and second is information on actual participation in Physical Education, Sports and Games. General discriptors for HPE are given for appraising a student on any specific activities, these general guidelines may be modified accordingly.

Sl.No.	*Descriptors*	*Score out of 5*
1.	Demonstrates physical fitness and agility	
2.	Displays courage and determination	
3.	Demonstrates flexibility of the body	
4.	Demonstrates sportsmanship	

(Contd...)

5.	Follows all safety norms of games and sports	
6.	Follows rules of the games	
7.	Has undergone training and coaching in the chosen sports and games items	
8.	Makes strategic decisions within the games	
9.	Organizes and provides leadership in this area	
10.	Takes initiative and interest in Physical Education and Wellness	
Total		
Average/Grade		

Participation and Performance: Instead of rating, the following information should be entered into student portfolio as descriptive statements. Choose any two of the following activities.

		Participation/Achievement Record			
Sl.No.	*Activities*	*Inter-class*	*Inter-school*	*Inter-district*	*Inter-state& beyond*
1.	Sports/Indigenous sports				
2.	NCC				
3.	NSS				
4.	Scouting and Guiding				
5.	Swimming				
6.	Gymnastics				
7.	Yoga				
8.	First Aid				
9.	Gardening				
10.	Shramdaan				

Annual Assessment: To reinforce day-to-day observation and quarterly behaviour rating, standardized tests and inventories will be administered either half-yearly or annually depending upon the attribute under assessment—

	Grade		*Grade Points*	
	A		4.1-5.0	
	B		3.1-4.0	
	C		2.1-3.0	
	D		1.1-2.0	
	E		0-1.0	

Each student will be graded on each of the 10 Life Skills, Work Education, Visual and Performing Arts, 03 Attitudes, Values, 02 Co-Curricular Activities and 02 Health and Physical Education (HPE) activities.

Maximum score for each Life Skill is 25, for Work Education, Visual and Performing Arts and Attitudes is 50, for Values is 200 and for Co-curricular Activities and HPE is 50.

Before assigning the Grades on each component using the conversion table, please calculate the average or grade points by dividing the total score obtained by a student by number of items in that component.

4

Tools and Techniques of Evaluation

There are two main purposes of evaluation. One is to provide development feedback to the learner, and the other is to qualitatively classify (grade) a learner on the basis of his/her learning outcome against a set of norms. Evaluation, hence, is an important decision making situation where a teacher is involved in a judgement. The quality of the decision depends on the quality of the data and information collected about the learner's learning accomplishments. In turn, quality of data and information depends upon the quality of tools and techniques of data gathering.

Hence, tools and techniques of evaluation are important components of the process of educational evaluation.

Interpretation of gathered information needs to be given in numerical scores, grades as well as in qualitative terms.

In educational evaluation, judgements should be made not just on scholastic aspects but also on co-scholastic aspects which depend to a large extent on the learning ambience and learning culture of an institution. As far as interpretation is concerned, attainment can be measured at different levels.

- With reference to the learner himself/herself—his/her current state of progress, strengths, learning gaps, etc.
- With reference to the criteria.the expected level of learning keeping in view the required skills

Tools are primarily instruments of collecting data and information. For example, questions, observations, tests, inventories, record or document analysis, etc. are tools. Tools, in the context of educational evaluation, require situations for application. For example, observation as a tool needs situations like debating competition, engagement in a project activity, etc. A teacher can observe a student while he is debating or working on a project, assignment or questions in a written examination.

Although it is difficult to precisely define and separate out tools from techniques, for the operational purposes of educational evaluation we may, classify situations which are occurring either naturally or contrived for assessment—as techniques.

Multiple tools can be used for assessment. Similarly, more than one assessment tool can be used in several assessment techniques. The Tools can be

- Standardized
- Non-standardized

Standardized tools have the attributes of objectivity, reliability, validity and quality of discriminating between a high and low performer. Different types of validities, e.g. construct, content and concurrent validity take care of balance, and relevance. Speed is a factor in some tests, but not a common element in all tests. Psychological tests and inventories like Intelligence and aptitude tests, Interest and study habit inventories, Attitude scales, etc. have those properties. Non standardized tools are teacher made tests, rating scale, observation schedules, interview schedules, questionnaire, opinionnaires, checklists, etc.

COMMONLY USED TESTS IN SCHOOLS

A teacher needs to be familiar with at least those tools which are commonly used in the school. Those tools help in the teaching-learning process. The two most commonly used tests in schools are diagnostic tests and achievement Tests.

Diagnostic Tests

Generally, we find that students have difficulties in understanding and learning certain concepts. The difficulties vary from individual to individual, subject to subject and class to class. In order to make the teaching-learning process effective, it is essential to find the learning difficulties of students during instruction. This can be done by making use of diagnostic tests. The diagnostic tests consist of items based on a detailed analysis of the specific skills involved in successful performance and a study of the most common errors made by students. The test difficulty is low. Thus, a good diagnostic test will permit a student to demonstrate all aspects of the skill being measured and will pinpoint the types of errors that he/she has made.

Diagnostic tests are available for different subjects. In order to select and use diagnostic tests, some different points to be kept in mind are:

1. While selecting a test, the diagnostic procedures should be evaluated in the light of the specific type of information desired.
2. Diagnostic tests are designed for students of below average performance in the particular subject(s). So they are useful in identifying weaknesses in

learning but not for indicating the level of proficiency. If a student scores high on a sub-test, it simply means that this student does not have, difficulties related to the area measured by the sub-test.

3. Diagnostic tests indicate the typical errors a student makes, but they do not indicate the causes of the errors. Some causes can be easily inferred from the type of error made, or from a student's explanation of how he/she arrived at the answer.
4. Diagnostic tests provide only partial information for diagnosing a student's difficulty. Other methods like observation have to be made use of to supplement and complement this information.
5. Results from diagnostic tests, concerning specific, learning difficulties, tend to have a low reliability because there are relatively few items measuring each type of error. Therefore, the findings regarding specific strengths and weaknesses for any particular pupil should be regarded as clues to be verified by other objective evidence and by regular classroom observation.

In conclusion, it may be said that a diagnostic test is a useful tool for analyzing learning difficulties. But in order to know the learning difficulties a diagnostic test alone may not be sufficient. Therefore, supplementary information concerning the physical, intellectual, social and emotional development of the student is also needed before an effective remedial programme can be initiated.

Achievement Tests

Achievement tests are generally classified as teacher-made tests and standardized tests. We normally use teacher-made tests in schools. Their results indicate student achievement in relation to the instructions provided in a school. These results are of great help in improving the teaching-learning process. They help the teachers in understanding their students, in taking proper decisions about teaching and testing the effectiveness of their own teaching. The students are motivated towards further learning and teachers, towards self-evaluation. Since instruction provided differs from school to school, the results of teacher-made tests cannot be compared. Teacher-made tests have some other drawbacks too. The scoring may not be objective and there is no standard procedure for its administration. There is no empirical evidence with respect to reliability and validity of teacher-made tests. Thus, they have limited utility.

Standardized Tests

A few standardized tests are available for some school subjects. Some characteristics of these tests are:

1. They consist of items of high quality. The items are pretested and selected on the basis of difficulty value, discrimination power, and relationship to clearly defined objectives in behavioural terms.
2. As the directions for administering, exact time limit, and scoring are precisely stated, any person can administer and score the test.
3. Norms, based on representative groups of individuals, are provided as an aid for interpreting the test scores. These norms are frequently based on age, grade, sex, etc.
4. Information needed for judging the value of the test is provided. Before the test becomes available, the reliability and validity are established.
5. A manual is supplied that explains the purposes and uses of the test, describes briefly how it was

constructed, provides specific directions for administering, scoring, and interpreting results, contains tables of norms, and summarizes available research data on the test.

No two standardized tests are exactly alike. Each test measures certain specific aspects of behaviour and serves a slightly different purpose. There are some tests with similar titles measuring aspects of behaviour that differ markedly, whereas other tests with dissimilar titles measure aspects of behaviour that are almost identical. Thus, one has to be careful in selecting a standardized test.

Standardized tests are sometimes used for evaluating the general educational development of students in the basic skills and in those learning outcomes common to many courses of study. They are also used for evaluating student progress during the school year or over a period of years and grouping students for instructional purposes. The purpose of diagnosing relative strengths and weaknesses of students in terms of broad subject or skill areas can also be achieved through the use of standardized tests.

Carefully constructed teacher-made tests and standardized tests are similar in many ways. Both are constructed on the basis of carefully planned table of specifications, both have the same type of test items, and both provide clear directions to the students. Still the two are differ. They differ in the quality of test items, the reliability of test measures, the procedures for administering and scoring and the interpretation of scores.

Teacher-made Vs. Standardized Achievement Tests

A comparison of teacher-made and standardized achievement tests is given in the table below:

Point of Comparison	*Teacher-made Achievement Test*	*Standardized Achievement Test*
1. Learning outcomes and content measured	They are used to evaluate the outcomes and content of what has been taught in the classroom.	They are used to evaluate outcomes and content that have been determined irrespective of what has been taught.
2. Quality of test items	Quality of test items unknown and is generally lower than items of standardized tests.	General quality of items is high. They are pretested and selected on the basis of difficulty and discrimination power.
3. Reliability	Reliability is usually unknown but it can be high if test items are carefully constructed.	Reliability is usually high.
4. Administration and scoring	Uniform procedure of administration and scoring may be possible. It is usually flexible.	The procedure of its administration is standardized and specific instructions for its administration and scoring are provided.
5. Interpretation of scores	Scores can be compared and interpreted only in the context of the local school situation.	Scores can be compared to norm groups, Test manuals and other guides for interpretation and use.

Both the teacher-made tests and standardized tests are used for some common and some different purposes. Standardized tests are useful when the purpose of testing is to compare a student's performance in different content areas; to find the status of an individual student, class, or school system in a wider population; to compare classes or schools among themselves; and to measure growth over a period of years. On the other hand, teacher-made tests are used to determine whether specific curriculum goals have been achieved, giving grades and comparing them with other students.

CHARACTERISTICS OF A GOOD EVALUATION TOOL

A good evaluation tools will have the following characteristics:

Validity

The validity of a test concerns what the test measures and how well it does so. If a test measures what it proclaims to measure, it is said to be valid; if it does not, it is invalid. Further, the validity of a test cannot be reported in broad terms. No test can be said to have "high" or "low" validity in general. Its validity must be determined with reference to the particular use for which the test is being considered.

Validity pertains to the measurement or result of a test, and not to the test. Sometimes one speaks of the validity of a test for the sake of convenience, but it is more appropriate to speak of the interpretation made from the result. Further, validity is a matter of degree. It is best considered in terms of categories that specify degree, such as high validity, moderate validity, and low validity.

Reliability

Reliability is the consistency of test scores or other evaluation results from one measurement to another. It his three characteristics. Firstly, reliability refers to the results obtained with an evaluation instrument, and not to the instrument itself as in the case of validity. Therefore, depending upon the group involved and the situation in which it is used, an instrument may have a number of reliabilities. Thus it is more appropriate to speak of the reliability of "the test scores" or "the measurement", than of "the test" or "the instrument". Secondly, an estimate of reliability refers to a particular type of consistency.

Test scores are not reliable in general. They are reliable over different periods of time, over different samples of questions, over different evaluations and so on and so forth. It is possible for test scores to be consistent in one of these respects and not in another. The appropriate type of consistency in a particular case is dictated by the use to be made of the result. Lastly, reliability is primarily statistical in nature. Logical analysis of a test will provide little evidence concerning the reliability of the scores. The test must be administered, one or more times, to a group of persons and only the consistency of the results can be determined. This consistency may be expressed in terms of shifts in the relative standing of persons in the group or in terms of the amount of variation to be expected in a particular individual's score.

Consistency of the first type is reported by means of a correlation coefficient called a reliability coefficient. Whereas consistency of the second type is reported by means of the standard error of measurement. Both these methods are widely used but they are primarily useful with norm-referenced measures.

Usability

While validity and reliability of a test are the most important factors to be considered in the choice of an appropriate measurement instrument for a given situation, its usability should also be considered. Sometimes a test must be eliminated from consideration because it is too long or too difficult to administer, or because the scoring procedure is too complex or the cost of administration too high. These and other factors must be considered in choosing an appropriate instrument.

Interpretation of Results

Another factor which must be considered in the choice of a test is the ease of interpretation of test results. A test score is not meaningful unless the teacher or counsellor is able to decide what significance or importance should be attached to it and to make some judgement concerning its relationship to other kind of information about the student. Nearly all test publishers produce manuals designed to aid the teacher in interpreting test results. But these manuals vary greatly on quality and in the thoroughness with which they do this important job. From the point of view of the teacher, principal, or counsellor, the quality of the test manual should be just as important a factor in the choice of a test as the quality of the test itself.

Format

In addition to the important factors of time, cost, ease of administration, ease of scoring, and case of interpretation, several other considerations in the evaluation of a measurement device should receive at least brief mention. Most of these have to do with the format of the test and the manner in which it is presented to the student. Since die test-taking experience may be inherently not so pleasant for the student, the test should be as attractive and interesting as possible. In evaluating the format, of a test there are several things that die teacher should look for:

1. Instructions indicating how the pupil is to record his/her answers to the items should be given on the test itself. These instructions should also include information concerning the scoring procedure that will be used.
2. In most cases the items should be arranged in order of difficulty, with die easier items presented first. Such an arrangement tends to encourage students to do their best on all items for which they have me necessary information or ability.
3. When possible, items should be grouped according to both format (true-false, multiple choice, etc.) and content. If this is done the student is less likely to mark incorrectly an item for which he/she really does have the required information.
4. The items should be arranged on the page so that they are easily readable. Complete item should be on the same page.
5. At least one practice example should be given at the beginning of each section of the test to familiarize the student with the format in that section.
6. The test manual should be available.

QUESTIONS

Questions are the most commonly applied assessment tool for finding out what children know, think, imagine, and feel. A teacher, in the course of teaching, comes to know of learning difficulties in children by asking questions. Questions as a tool are primarily used in examinations.

Characteristics of a Good Question

(i) *Objective based:* A question should be based on a pre-determined objective and should be framed in such a way that it tests the objective effectively.

(ii) *Instructions:* It should specify a particular task through the instructions. For this, appropriate directional words should be used and structured situations should be given.

(iii) *Scope:* It should indicate the limit and the scope of the answer (length of the answer) in accordance with the estimated time and marks allotted to it.

(iv) *Content:* The question should assess the same area of content which it intends to assess.

(v) *Language:* A good question is framed in a clear, precise and unambiguous language, well within the comprehension of the students.

(vi) *Difficulty level:* A question should be written keeping in view the level of the students for whom it is meant. The difficulty of the question depends upon the ability to be tested, content area to be tested and the time available to answer it.

(vii) *Assessing power*: A good question must assess between the bright students and the other students.

(viii) *Delimited scope of the answer*: The language of the question should be specific and precise so that the scope of the expected answer is clearly delimited or defined.

(ix) *Value points*: Value points or marks carried by a question as a whole and also its sub parts should be clearly mentioned.

Form of Questions

The form of question depends on the objective and the content area to be tested. Some forms are better than the others for testing certain abilities. A good question paper should have the questions based on:

(i) Remembering—e.g. How many...?, Can you name...?, Who spoke to...?, What happened after?

(ii) Understanding—e.g. How would you explain...?, Who do you think...?, Can you clarify....?

(iii) Applying—e.g. Which factors would you change if...?, From the information given, can you develop a set of instructions about...?, Do you know of another instance where...? Etc.

(iv) Analysing—e.g. Which events could not have happened...?, How is ... similar to...?, Why did....changes occur?, What was the turning point?, What was the problem with...?

(v) Evaluating—e.g. Is there a better solution to...?, What are the alternatives...?, What are the pros and cons of...?, How effective are...?, Do you think ...is a good or bad thing?

(vi) Creating—e.g. Can you design a....to...?, What would happen if...?, Can you see a possible solution to...?, Can you develop a proposal which would..?

Types of Questions

The answer may vary from one word to several

paragraphs. Such type of questions are also called as 'free-response' questions. Supply-type questions may be divided into four categories as follows:

(i) Essay

(ii) Short answer

(iii) Very short answer

(iv) Objective type

Essay Type Questions

The term essay implies a written response which is a sustained form of writing. The student is allowed to have freedom with respect to wording, length and organization of the answer. A distinction should be made between the essay type question used to measure knowledge and the essay type question employed to test writing skills in languages which is called a writing task.

There are many abilities which may not be tested through any other form of question but only by the essay type question. These abilities are:

- Select relevant facts from the body of acquired knowledge
- Identify and also establish relationships between various aspects of knowledge
- Weigh the proof with respect to implications of the gathered information
- To organize, analyse, interpret facts and other types of information to draw inferences
- Adopt an indigenous or original approach to solve a given problem
- Defend one's point of view through facts, data and suitable arguments

- Critically examine the degree of adequacy, accuracy and relevance of the available information in a given situation
- Appreciate a problem at both the macro and micro levels
- Conceive, design and suggest new and innovative approaches for tackling a given problem.

Constructing Essay Type Questions

Essay type questions usually begin with such terms as 'discuss', 'explain', 'evaluate', 'define', 'compare', 'contrast', 'describe', etc. Essay type questions are good when the group to be tested is small and limited time is available for test preparation. It is also quite suitable to test written expression.

Some sample essay type questions are:

(a) Why do sandy soils not hold enough water? (Question Form)

(b) Explain any of the four sense organs and draw their diagrams (Statement Type)

Compare both the questions:

- Give reasons why Roosevelt won the 1932 presidential election in the USA
- The most important reason why Roosevelt won the 1932 presidential election was Hoover's unpopularity. Do you agree? Explain your answer.

You will notice that:

- The first encourages rote-learning and does not call upon the skills of independent thoughts, analysis and evaluation required. The second assumes vital importance for all and not simply the gifted few.

Short Answer Questions

Essay type questions suffer from lack of objectivity and reliability while objective type questions cannot be used for testing certain aspects of growth like the ability to express, summarise and organize the ideas in a precise manner. Short answer questions are a good via-media between the two extremes. If understood and framed properly, they have the advantages of both the objective type and essay type questions.

Some characteristics of short answer questions are:

- Short answer questions can be used profitably in all tests
- It can be used to test almost all the objectives of teaching
- It helps students to develop the ability of organising and selecting relevant facts
- It can be scored more objectively than the essay type questions and thereby ensure reliability
- These questions help in covering more syllabus because more number of questions can be put in lieu of one-essay type question. This improves the validity of the question paper.

Very Short Answer Questions

Characteristics of short answer questions are:

- Very short answer questions are those which have one specific testing point and can be marked quite objectively
- More content can be tested through these questions and more reliability and validity can be ensured
- It helps in testing knowledge of the examinee by asking him to supply a word, phrase, figure or a

sentence which is required for answering the questions

- It can be answered in one word to one sentence
- It mostly takes one to two minutes to answer and the mark allotted may be one mark
- Very short answer questions can be used profitably in all the school subjects.

Objective Type Questions

In these type of questions students have to answer them by selecting the correct answer among the provided choices. These may be divided into alternative response type, matching type and multiple choice type questions, etc.

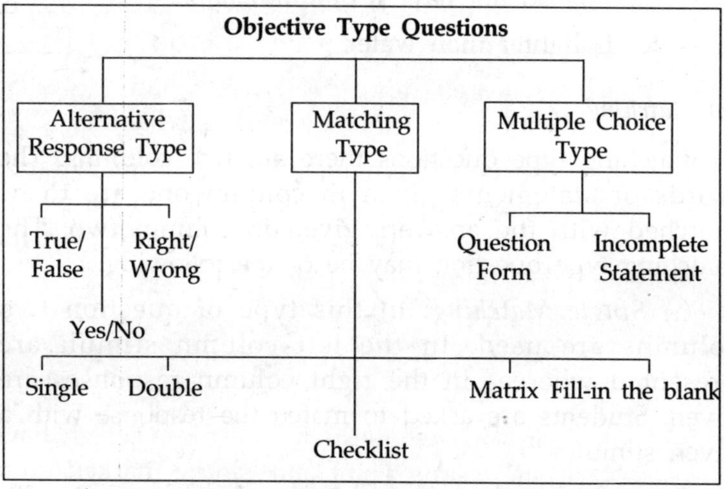

Some examples of each type of question is mentioned under each head:

(a) Alternative Response Type

In these type of questions students have to select one out

of two alternatives as a correct answer. The different type of alternative response questions are as under:

(i) *True-False or Yes-No Question:* In this type of question a statement is given and the candidate is asked whether it is true or false (T/F). True/False questions are easy to construct and score. They provide a fairly reliable measure of students understanding particularly in the classroom testing.

Example:

– Both animals and plants are living things ☐

– All animals eat small animals ☐

(ii) Right/Wrong Type or Yes/No Type: Put tick (✔) mark if statement is Right and (x) if Wrong.

– Liquids do not have a definite shape ☐

– Ice is lighter than water ☐

(b) Matching

In matching type questions there are two columns. The words or statements given in column one are to be matched with the answers given in column two. The matching type question may be of the following:

(i) *Single Matching*: In this type of question two columns are used. In the left column stimuli are presented whereas in the right column responses are given. Students are asked to match the response with a given stimulus.

Example: Match the words given in Column A with Column B to make a correct pair. (Simple type)

Sl. No.	*Column A*	*Column B*
1	Morning	Stars
2	Night	24 hours
3	Day	Sun light

Example: Match the words given in column A with the meanings given in column B. (Difficult type)

A	B
Barber	One who makes bread/biscuits, etc.
Waiter	One who is incharge of a place
Baker	One who cuts people's hair
Architect	One who serves food in a hotel
Caretaker	One who designs buildings, bridges etc.

(ii) *Double Matching*: In this type of item, one list of stimuli is provided to test two areas of knowledge. So three columns are used instead of two columns. In the middle column, stimuli and in both left and right columns, two sets of responses are provided.

- There are three columns i.e. I, II and III. In the column II there is a list of four animals while the Column I provides animal behaviour and Column III gives the type of foods they usually eat.

  Put appropriate letter and number in Column I and III.

Column I (Behaviour)	*Column II (Animal)*	*Column III (Food)*
1. Likes daylight but active at night	*(a)* Rat	A. Live insects
2. Likes daylight and active during the day	*(b)* Moth	B. Flower nectar
3. Does not like daylight	*(c)* House Fly	C. Flesh of animals
4. Does not like day light but active in day and night	*(d)* Lizard	D. Plant leaves
		E. Bread
		F. Load of organic matter
		G. Wood
		H. Snakes

(iii)) *Checklist*: In this type of item, students are provided two or three alternatives as the checklist to make decisions about a number of statements on the basis of the checklist provided.

Advantages of Checklist:

- Quick and easy to implement
- Provides specific information about specific objectives
- Can point towards a trend of how and when skills have been acquired by the student as well as a group of students?

Concerns Regarding Checklist:

- Limited information only indicating presence of a skill
- Does not indicate student's response to different situations or provide specific examples of responses?
- Does not provide information about context?
- Can at times become unwieldy because of the number of specific items?

Suggestion for implementation of Checklist:

- Add a 'comments' column to add value to the information in the checklist marking
- Use this tool in conjunction with other methods of assessments
- If developed by others, a checklist may not be suitable for the objectives that you as teachers have in mind or for the groups, you wish to use it with
- An excellent way of finding, recording specific behaviour, action, processes, outcomes, approaches, problems and helps to focus attention on particular aspects of evaluation.

Example: For each of the following matters use letters to indicate whether the matter is a Solid (S)/ Liquid (L)/ Gas (G).

Matter	*State*
1. Water	
2. Mercury	
3. Vapour	
4. Iron	

(iv) *Matrix:* These are extensions of double matching type items wherein more than two responses are linked to a stimuli. In such type of items, stimuli are presented vertically (in row) wherein responses are presented horizontally (in columns). Students are asked to check each cell in which the response on the top is true for each of the stimuli along the side.

Deficiency can cause

Vitamins	Excessive Bleeding (1)	Beriberi (2)	Rickets (3)	Anemia (4)	Scurvy (5)	Night blindness (6)
A						
B_{11}						
B_{12}						
C						
D						
K						

(v) *Fill in the Blanks Type*: In this type of question, a statement is provided in which one word or two words at different places are removed and students are asked to fill in the blanks with appropriate words. An example of this type is given below:

(*a*) Leaves give out water vapour through the process of..................................(transpiration/photosynthesis)

(*b*) Motion in a straight line is called...................motion (rectilinear/periodic).

(c) Multiple Choice

Multiple choice questions are the most useful of all the objective type items. In these questions, there is a stem which poses the problem. The stem may be in question form or in the form of an incomplete statement. Then there are four or five choices given for an answer. The student has to select the correct answer from the given alternatives. On the basis of the stem, multiple choice questions may be of two types.

(*i*) *Question Form*: (Testing instructional objective-interpretation)

Which one of the following diseases is a non-infectious disease?

(*i*) Small pox (*ii*) Heart attack (*iii*) Malaria (*iv*) Cholera

(*ii*) *Incomplete Statement Form*: (Testing instructional objectives—Identify relationships)

The character shared by the whale and a bat is the possession of

(*i*) Hair (*ii*) Wings (*iii*) Limbs (*iv*) Neck

The forms of questions discussed above may be used for different purposes of testing and also making judgement regarding the achievement of the students. If in a test, more varieties of the question forms are used then it will definitely help in testing various objectives and content areas in a better way on one hand and also making it a more reliable and valid instrument on the other hand. It is true that though different forms have some Limitations, they do have advantages over each other. Therefore, at the time of the selection of forms all aspects should remain in the mind of teachers so that these forms may be exploited for their best use.

(iii) *Completion Type*: It is useful for testing expression in language testing.

Q. I was so worried...

(iv) *Analogy type*:

Q. What lime stone is to marble, coal is tod..............

(v) *Location Type*: In Geography such questions can be used for testing map skills.

Q. Show on the map—China, Sahara Desert.

In language also such questions can be used for picking up the key ideas, key words or sentences, synonyms and antonyms etc. from the given passage.

(vi) *Transformation Type:* This type is used only in language testing. Reported speech, voices, synthesis, transformation of sentences, etc. can be tested through this type of question.

(vii) *Interpretive Type:* Read the bus time table given below and answer the questions that follow:

Himachal Pradesh Roadways Bus Service Time Table

Route	*Dep. Time from Delhi*	*Dep. Time from Other direction*	*Distance (in Km.)*	*Fare (in Rs.)*
Delhi-Baijnath	1815	1730	539	77.00
Delhi-Chamba	2000	1400	626	84.00
Delhi-Dharamsala	2145	1930	513	71.50

— What is the title of the bus time table?

— How many routes are listed in the time table?

CHARACTERISTICS OF A GOOD QUESTION PAPER

Far from being a random assemblage of questions, setting of a good question paper is a highly developed technique. The question paper is balanced with respect to several factors which are considered to be significant from the point of view of assessing performance of students with a high degree of validity and reliability. The major task of a question paper is that it should discriminate the low achievers from the high achievers and be able to place the students at their correct relative position within the group in accordance with the degree of proficiency attained by them. In this process, testing of various faculties/abilities of the learners, intensive coverage of the subject matter (areas of the syllabus), quality of individual questions, types of responses they elicit, task set for the students, general level of performance expected in the question paper and several such factors acquire a special significance. In fact, these are the pre-considerations which should go into every question paper if it has to perform its pre-conceived functions well. Indeed, each question set is a creative work and assemblage of such questions according to a pre-conceived plan an art.

Defects of a Traditional Question Paper

The construction of a good question paper requires a great deal of planning prior to the actual writing of questions. Good questions do not just happen nor are they the result of a few moments of high inspiration. On the contrary, the process is calm, deliberate and time consuming. Knowledge of the defects of the traditional question papers, which teachers have been generally using may help in the construction of a good question paper. Some of the defects of the traditional question papers are listed below:

(i) The limited number of questions which mostly require recall of information and encourage memorisation on the part of the students do not adequately cover all the topics of the syllabus or different aspects of a topic and do not test the high abilities like understanding, application and skill.

(ii) Directional words like "Explain", "Interpret", "what do you know", "Give an account of", "write short notes on" etc. make a question paper vague. The students, very often, cannot determine what answers are required. The examiners themselves are not clear about the nature of the answers required by the students. Marks allotted by different examiners for similar answers, therefore, vary appreciably and hence evaluation of students' performance in the examination is defective.

(iii) Most of the questions are generally stereotyped, textbook oriented and essay type. As a result, these questions are inadequate to assess the real abilities of students in problem-solving. Since essay type questions may be very few in number, large portions of the syllabus are left uncovered. This leads to the guessing of expected questions and preparation of set answers which become the main learning effort for the examinees.

(iv) Options are very often provided, stating that all questions carry equal marks and the students may attempt any five or six out of ten or more (or less) questions. This again provides students with freedom to prepare only selected important topics and leave out the rest without any serious risk.

(v) There is overemphasis on calculation and mechanical manipulation of figures and symbols. Certain aspects of mathematical knowledge and their application are not tapped at all by the questions.

(vi) Sometimes questions are so framed that the answers are not unique.

Question Bank

Banking is the process of retaining of examination questions, tests or other assessment material and reusing them for other sets of students in subsequent years. Banking is most commonly used for objective questions, but it can and should be used for other assessment methods also.

The question bank is a planned library of test items to be used by evaluators, teachers and students in partial fulfilment of the requirements of the teaching-learning process. It is not a haphazard collection of a number of questions. The question bank is designed to fulfil certain pre-determined purposes. Its efficient functioning demands cooperative enterprise. Its focus is on improvement of the teaching-learning process. Its clientele is specified, depending upon the nature arid scope of die questions that constitute die bank. It is a utility service with an inbuilt feedback mechanism for improvement of its questions.

A question bank can serve two purposes—to enrich the instructional side as well as to judge the pupil's growth in terms of instructional efforts. On the instructional side, questions can be used by teachers at die pre-testing stage, for the development of a lesson and for revision of home assignments. A pool of test questions on a unit or a topic can be used for formative evaluation which is an integral part of teaching. Such a stock of questions can also be made use of, in preparing question papers at die end of a term or a session for summative evaluation. Questions can also be used for diagnosis of the pupil's difficulties.

There are a number of reasons why banking is recommended:

(*a*) Good examination questions and assessment tasks are difficult to set and much work goes, or should go, into their preparation. It is, therefore, wasteful to discard them after a single use.

(*b*) Most courses contain at least some material which needs to be tested fairly frequently, if not every year. Questions on these topics are likely to resemble one another greatly, even if there is no banking, so that little is gained by the attempt to set fresh questions.

(*c*) Banking is usually associated with statistical analysis of the assessment and its component questions or tasks; analysis helps to show how satisfactory the assessment has been and how subsequent assessments can be improved.

(*d*) Banking of analysed questions is the best means of ensuring the comparability of standards from year to year. It is possible to compare die performance of two groups of students on questions or tasks which they both attempted.

Not everything can be banked successfully, though most forms of assessment can be.

(*a*) Objective questions can be banked individually.

(*b*) Short answer and structured questions can be banked provided that they are accompanied by a good marking scheme.

(*c*) Essay questions are probably not worth banking, as the marking is unlikely to be reliable enough to allow comparison of results from year to year.

(d) Whole tests can be banked. This involves much less work than banking questions singly, but it does make it more important to preserve the security of the bank. Also, it is most improbable that a test will prove to be perfect the first time that it is used. So, at least initially, it will be necessary to modify the tests before giving them a place in the bank. An easier alternative might be to bank pages of tests, each containing questions for one syllabus section.

(e) Practical examinations, phased practical tests and their component parts can quite readily be banked.

(f) Assignments can be banked.

(g) Projects can sometimes be banked, but there is a danger that the problems involved may become known and discussed. Projects are not normally held under examination condition and student's project work may well be returned to them. So security is difficult to achieve. However the drawings or other material on which the-project is based should certainly be retained, as they may form the basis of a second project requiring the student to carry out rather different tasks.

(h) Any tests or exercises set as part of assessment may be banked. It will help to ensure consistency of standards.

ORAL TESTS

Oral examination is a time-honoured form of measurement. It is still used at the university level for thesis examinations, at the early childhood level for content examinations, and at the post-school level for occupational placement examination. However, for many measurement purposes the oral examination is seldom used. Its fall from favour is a result of the many structural weaknesses in the oral examination format.

In the classical form of the oral examination, the question is presented orally to the examinee and is responded to in like manner. However, two alternative forms of response to orally presented problems (written and performance) should also be considered because they have elements in common with the more traditional oral response form.

Oral Response Test

In the oral-response form of the oral examination, the examiner presents the questions using the spoken word and the examinee responds in the same manner. This type of test is considered by many to be the only legitimate form of oral examination.

Advantages

The advantages attributed to the oral-response test are due primarily to the somewhat unique characteristics of this test form: it is presented orally and responded to orally. Therefore, the reading level and writing ability of the examinee are not involved in the examination. This contributes to the overall flexibility of oral-response examinations. They can be used in many situations appropriate to other types of tests and in some unique situations where other tests are inappropriate.

Disadvantages

There are several severe disadvantages associated with the oral-response test. Whether the test is administered in a classroom setting or in a cubicle with only the examiner and the examinee present, it is basically an individual examination restricted to the verbal interaction of examiner and examinee for any one question. Also the administration of an oral-response test is exceedingly time-consuming, especially when it involves in-depth questioning. Of all the methods available for the collection of test data, this is the least efficient.

Written Response Test

In the written-response form of the oral examination, the questions are presented by the examiner by the use of the spoken word and are answered in writing by the examinee. The written-response test can be thought of as falling somewhere between the classical oral examination (oral-response) and the written examination. Whether it is closer to the oral-response test or the written test depends primarily on the purpose for using this particular test form.

Disadvantages

In the written-response form of the oral-examination, many of the advantages of the oral response test do not apply. Since the examinees must be able to write, skill in writing tends to become a part of the score given to a response. It is seldom appropriate for use with the young child or with the physically handicapped who lack writing skills. Furthermore, the opportunity to probe in depth in selected areas at the discretion of the examiner is lost. In addition, it is of little use in measuring oral communication skills. The written response form lacks most of the unique advantages of the more traditional oral examination except for a few instructional objectives which are amenable to written tests.

Advantages

The written-response form of the oral examination is used by the classroom teacher more often than the oral-response form. Since it can be used to examine several students simultaneously, rather than only one at a time, many of the defects of the oral-response test are less significant for this test form. For example, all examinees have the opportunity to respond to every item, thus providing a common criterion for comparing responses.

Furthermore, unless the examinees are privately quizzed, in a given amount of testing time, each examinee can be asked more questions in the written-response test than in the oral-response test.

There are there situations in which this form of the oral examination may prove to be more appropriate than its written examination counterpart: (1) where there is a shortage of resources needed to reproduce the tests; (2) when auditory comprehension is an integral part of the test; and (3) when it is difficult to write questions to measure instructional objectives which can be measured by oral examination items more easily. For example, spelling skill can be measured by the teacher pronouncing the words and the students writing them on a sheet of paper.

Oral Performance Test

In the performance test, the student is orally presented with a task to carry out, and his/her skill in executing it is assessed. Many instructional objectives which cannot be measured by written tests are amenable to measurement by oral examinations of the performance variety.

Oral performance tests are particularly well suited to the languages and related areas. For example, students may be required to translate a passage read out to them into a foreign language, carry on a brief and controlled conversation in a foreign language with an examiner, or transcribe in shorthand a letter dictated to them.

In the past, teachers gave frequent oral examinations by having students stand up by their seats and recite the lessons they had studied. This technique is less often used today because of the development of group discussion techniques and evaluation by means of short answer tests. However, oral questioning is a good way to discover what thought processes a pupil uses in solving problems.

In the pre-school, kindergarten, and lower primary grades the oral examination is probably the only way to evaluate achievement because the pupils have not yet learned to read. In higher grades oral examinations are often desirable when the teacher wishes to evaluate a student's ability to discuss broad types of problems in which integration of knowledge in several areas is important. These examinations also have some value as a diagnostic tool in situations where written tests or product and procedure techniques cannot be used.

On the adverse side, oral examinations have the same limitations as essay examinations—poor sampling of content, great consumption of time, and low reliability. They certainly cannot by themselves provide a satisfactory basis for determining grades for a pupil's work in a given area of instruction.

PRACTICAL TESTS

One of the most important features of teaching in schools has been the tradition of practical work carried out by individual pupils; this characteristic has been particularly evident in respect of the teaching of science subjects or vocational subjects like typing, tailoring, etc. It also plays an important role in professional courses like Medicine, Engineering and in Technical education. Practical work has been seen to constitute an important element in the teaching-learning process and the development of practical skill has been established as an important desirable outcome of courses in many subjects.

You will find that some practical work is carried out in a teaching course with the purpose of introducing, developing or reinforcing theoretical concepts; such work might be regarded as being relatively unimportant by some, but it has its own importance in the teaching-learning process.

Some subjects are often described as practical subjects. For instance, Art and Craft subjects as for example needlework and dressmaking, cookery, woodwork and metalwork. This description usually indicates that one of the major educational objectives of the course of study is the acquisition and development of certain practical skills. In science subjects such as Physics, Chemistry and Biology, practical work is of importance in establishing and illustrating the theoretical aspects of the subject as well as developing necessary and desirable skills which all students of the subject should be required to possess.

Practical work involves the application of knowledge, the use of theoretical concepts and the theoretical evaluation of the results obtained by the practical experience. All such inter-relationships between practice and theory raise problems for effective assessment.

Skill in Observation

The purpose of the assessment here is to measure the extent to which in any given situation the student observes those things which should be observed and makes appropriate interpretations in order that he/she can subsequently evaluate the results of these observations. Pupils can be presented with specific observations either as demonstrations or as exercises to carry out themselves, and be required to make their records of what has happened. The assessment will leair heavily on the ability of the student to report his/her observations and it is inevitable that the assessment will often take the form of awarding marks for written records of observation.

Information about a child (his/her behaviour) can be collected in 'natural' settings in and outside the class through observation. Other information can be collected through planned and purposeful observation of students during activities and tasks.

Advantages of Observation

- Recognize and identify the various aspects of students' personality development
- Recognize and identify the individuals as well as groups
- Recognize and identify on a continuing basis at varying time periods
- Recognize and identify the students' performance and knowledge based on an 'on-the-spot record'
- Over time, a pattern of interests, aptitudes etc. emerge creating a comprehensive picture of the student.

Concerns and risks in Observation as an assessment tool

- Jumping to conclusions based on one or few observations
- Skill of the observer determining 'what' is observed
- Lack of sensitivity and objectivity in the way the observation is done
- Observations in one situation and not across time and different activities and settings.

Observations can be used as a tool of assessment in a variety of situations. Techniques like debates, elocution, group work, practical and laboratory activities, projects, in play fields and school prayers, in clubs and festivals can be used. Whereas observation can be biased and subjective, such errors and risks can be substantially reduced by using an observation schedule.

Here are sample observation schedules in debates, group discussion, practical works in laboratory and projects.

(i) Debate: Sample observation criteria

Each observation can be assigned a score out of five.

No.	Descriptors	Score out of 5
1	Depth of knowledge of the content	
2	Strength of the argument to convince	
3	Fluency, diction and pronunciation	
4	Ability to contradict a given point of view	
5	Ability to take criticism positively	
6	Respectful to the opponent	
7	Body language while arguing	

(ii) Group Discussion:

Sample observation criteria Each observation can be assigned a score out of five

No.	Descriptors	Score out of 5
1	Contributes to the discussion	
2	Knowledgeable about the subject of discussion	
3	Involves others in the discussion	
4	Demonstrates leadership skills	
5	Accepts criticism positively	
6	Contributes creative ideas	
7	Carefully listens to others	

(iii) Practical/Lab Activity:

A few sample observation criteria that can be assigned a score out of five

No.	Descriptors	Score out of 5
1	Sets up experiments (right apparatus) carefully and properly	
2	Uses the appropriate technique to perform the experiment	
3	Collects data and observations correctly	
4	Works with precision, neatness and accuracy	

5	Interprets data, observation and draws inferences correctly	
6	Relates the findings with theoretical knowledge	
7	Demonstrates in-depth knowledge during viva	

(iv) Projects

As projects are carried for completion over a period of time, it provides significant opportunity to assess both Scholastic and Co-Scholastic skills of students. A few sample observation criteria that can be assigned a score out of five

No.	*Descriptors*	*Score out of 5*
1	Has done enough research and collected relevant information	
2	Reflects creativity and aesthetic skills	
3	Demonstrates understanding of the concept in the project documentation	
4	Consults internet and other material in completing the project	
5	Has he/she conducted any interviews regarding the project	
6	Demonstrates originality in the approach to the project	
7	Has interpreted results appropriately	

The Ability to Assess and Interpret the Data Obtained from Practical(s)

Here the purpose of the assessment is to measure the extent to which the student can evaluate the results obtained by practical work. This quality involves the application of factual and theoretical knowledge to a specific situation and the use which the pupil makes of his/her observations and recordings.

Several levels of activity can be included under this general heading. The student can be required to carry out calculations to identify something unknown, or to determine particular characteristics of the material under practical investigation. The student could also be required to interpret the results of a particular piece of practical work in the light of other practical experience and to relate different experiences to the particular situation with which he/she is faced.

Many practical examinations require the students to draw conclusions from practical work. This requires an explanation of the processes involved or a development of the situation, or both.

CHECKLIST

The concept of checklist has been provided earlier under questions. However, checklists can be used in several other areas of assessment. For example, as a part of Life Skills, whether a student can dress up neatly suitable to the occasion or a student can confidently address the students during the school prayer. Checklist is used where answer is in either 'yes' or 'no'. There may be a possibility of confusion. Checklists can be filled only by collecting the information by observing or questioning or by document analysis. Hence, checklist is primarily an instrument of data recording and documentation.

RATING SCALE

Rating scale is used wherever a response or a learner behaviour is likely to be in a continuum—from excellent to bad or from satisfactory to unsatisfactory.

ANECDOTAL RECORDS

Anecdotal records derives its origin and meaning from the word 'anecdotes'—brief events and episodes. An Anecdotal Record is the observed behaviour of a student. It is a record of some significant episode in the life of the student that sheds light on the conduct, thinking, skills and capabilities revealing significant features and characteristics about his/her personality.

In order to arrive at a trend or pattern, emphasis is on recording multiple episodes or anecdotes. Every time, a teacher documents an episode or an anecdote, she records her comments too.

Preparation of Anecdotal Records

We cannot set any limit on the number of anecdotes to be recorded. It depends upon the time which is at the disposal of the teachers or counsellors. The following points should be considered in connection with these records:

- These supplement other records and should not be considered as substitutes
- The objective description of the behaviour should not be mixed up with the subjective comments
- Any significant behaviour, be it in the classroom, in the school or outside the school, should be recorded
- Student's behaviour, whether it is favourable, unfavourable or neither of the two should be recorded
- The facts presented in all the anecdotes must be shifted and arranged so that they may be studied in relation to one another
- The record should be regarded as confidential. It should not fall into irresponsible hands.

Specimen of an Anecdotal Record

Name of the school:	
Name of the student observed:	Class:
Observer:	Date and Place:
Objective Description:	Comments of the Observer:

Uses of Anecdotal Records

- They provide specific description of personality and minimize generalizations
- They are very helpful in understanding the child's behaviour in diverse situations
- They provide a continuous record
- They provide data for learners to use in self-appraisal
- A summary of these records is valuable when forwarding a student record
- The new members of the staff may use these records and acquaint themselves with the student body
- These records aid in clinical service
- They motivate teachers to use the records.

DOCUMENT ANALYSIS

Record or document analysis is extensively used in research. The significance of this technique is with regard to assessment of students on the basis of documents, e.g. assignments, projects, journals in science, geography, etc. In a way, this technique is also used to evaluate answers to essay type questions. The assessor, here, searches and identifies the main points, arguments, illustrations and examples, derivations and numerals to justify the concept and its explanation, etc.

PORTFOLIO

It is the collection of evidences of students' work over a period of time. It could be day-to-day work or selection of the learner's best piece of work. Painters and commercial artists often use Portfolios to demonstrate their skills and quality work before the selection committees.

Advantages of Portfolio

– Provides a cumulative record of growth and development of a skill or competence in an area over a period of time.

– Enables a student to demonstrate to others, his/her learning and progress.

– Student becomes an active participant in the learning and assessment process.

Concern regarding Portfolio

– Selected work to be put into the Portfolio, should have a specific reason.

– Not all papers/items of work are to be included. This will become unmanageable.

Suggestions for implementation of Portfolio

– Student should be encouraged to participate in selection of Portfolio contents as well as in developing the criteria for selection of the contents.

– Continuous updating of the Portfolio as the child grows.

– Careful structuring of Portfolio material accompanied by a reflective account.

– Clear labelling and numbering of content for easy reference.

Portfolio can include

– *Photographs*: Provides an insight into the child's emotional, social and psychological aspects of development.

— *Paintings and other examples of artistic endeavour*: Provides evidence of a learner's abilities, thoughts and attitudes.
— *Audio-Video Recordings*: Specific situation or over a time span to cover important processes and aspects that can be recorded and analyzed later.
— *Self-Assessment Sheets:* Portfolio to provide evidence of the learner's self evaluation.
— *Peer Assessment Sheets:* Excellent for assessing in team and group based activities, social projects and peer related behaviour. Can be incorporated into the learner's Portfolio to provide evidence of the learner's social Life skills.
— *Parent Assessment Sheets*: Can be incorporated into the learner's Portfolio to provide evidence of evaluation done by the parent.

QUIZZES, COMPETITIONS

Quizzes and competitions are quite commonplace activities today in electronic media, TV in particular. This kind of assessment usually turns out to be joyful. Besides testing the knowledge of the participants, it helps in building collaboration and team work in group events.

ASSIGNMENTS

Theme based tasks to be completed as class work or homework and can be open ended or structured. Some could be based on contexts outside textbooks.

Advantages

— Provides students an opportunity to search for information, construct their own ideas, and articulate the same ideas through spoken, written and visual expressions

- Helps assess a wide range of objectives and content of learning.
- Provides students an opportunity to relate and synthesize within and outside school learning.

Caution for teachers

- Not too much homework, assignments or class work should be given which is currently the practice.
- Assignments should be such that they can be managed by students on their own.
- Should not become the only method of assessment.

Suggestions for implementation

- Going beyond collection of assignments by following it up with analysis, discussion and reflection
- Creativity of students is promoted
- Encouraging students to go beyond the textbooks
- Group work is to be encouraged.

EVALUATION: IMPLICATIONS FOR SCHOOLS

Role of Teachers

The examination system is complex. It has to meet the requirements and expectations of stakeholders at different levels and perform multiplicity of functions. The purpose of an examination may variously be one of certification, of selection, of institutional accountability, or an instrument of social change. More often it is indeed an amalgam of many functions. Those who engage in educational reform must take account of the full range of stakeholder requirements and ensure that a degree of coherence in those expectations has been achieved.

Reforms which encourage School Based Assessment, create new pressures of accountability and place greater reliance on the professional judgement of teachers. Pedagogies which work in one educational context, perhaps with more generous resourcing levels and optimum class sizes are not necessarily transposable into other contexts. A rich dialogue between policy makers and teachers is required to ensure its effective implementation. Opportunities for professional development, in-service training and guidance via the production of exemplar materials and handbooks become vital. Educational reforms which call for new pedagogies, the incorporation of ICT into the curriculum for the encouragement of e-learning are possible only by an unwavering commitment to the training programmes for teachers.

Modes of assessment emphasize investigative approaches to learning and the application of skills, knowledge and understanding. The approach recognizes that 'recall' becomes a relatively less useful skill for individuals in today's world of rapid change. Instead understanding, applying, analyzing, evaluating and creating, the higher order thinking skills (HOTS) of a reworked Bloom's taxonomy become more relevant.

Of all those involved in student's education, it is the teachers who feel the most responsible. This is expressed in their desire to help all children acquire knowledge, skills, positive attitudes and values and face life with confidence. In order to find out how students are doing in school, teachers spend a lot of time in assessing students. Most teachers view assessment as an important part in their daily school routine. Why is this so? Teachers give a number of reasons for this. One important reason is that it is necessary to know if the student has learnt what she/he was expected to have learnt. The second is to find out what the student's progress has been over a certain period of time. However, there is a third reason that has been given more attention by not only the teachers but all of us as well i.e. finding out what the student has achieved in different subject areas. This could be because we are all concerned about providing 'good quality' education and feel that one way of making sure this is happening is by evaluating the student's achievement in the subjects being taught through tests and exams.

Testing has its own purpose but if we really want to help students learn better, we need to consider what marks or grades obtained by children through tests or exams actually tell us about a child's learning or progress. While assessing students, it is important to appreciate differences amongst them and respect the fact that they will understand and respond in different ways while learning. Students are not 'empty vessels' or 'blank slates', to be filled up with information and knowledge that only the school can give, as is generally believed. It is important to build experiences which a student brings to the school. New learning needs to be based on what the student already knows and understands.

Some important aspects are:

- Every student can learn if allowed to do so at her/his own pace and follow her/his own way of learning
- Students learn more through play and activities and learn better from each other and if they actually 'do' things
- Learning is a continuous process. Thus, student's learning does not take place in the school. Therefore, classroom learning should be linked to what happens outside the classroom and at home.
- Students 'construct' their own knowledge and do not only learn when and what the teacher teaches.

This means that every student makes sense of what information he/she is exposed to based on his/her previous experiences and learning. Only then does the student arrive at his/her own understanding and conclusions. Each child has a unique approach to acquiring knowledge. And this is a continuous process.

— Students at the primary stage learn better and more easily through experiences, play, exploration, trying out various things and actually 'doing' different activities.

— Students learn in a spiral and not a linear way. Thus, revisiting concepts again and again helps them to understand better. The act of learning involves a process of establishing connections among facts observed and experienced by students. The new learning, therefore, is to be based not only on the preceding facts and information but could be related even to things acquired long back in school, home or elsewhere. Hence, learning does not proceed in a linear manner.

— Students learn through the mistakes and errors they make themselves.

— Learning takes place in a holistic manner, thus, an integrated approach to learning is better.

Assessment

Assessment of the outcomes of learning goes along with the teaching-learning process in a continuous manner. In order to undertake a holistic assessment, all aspects of learning need to be given due recognition. The manner and modalities however may vary. While teachers are regularly observing the progress of students some periodicity would be necessary. It implies maintaining a profile for each student. This is required in order to reflect upon, derive feedback, plan and implement measures to enrich and enhance student's learning. This will call for a judicious cycle to be followed. One cannot undermine the fact that while informal observations continue, fortnightly looking back and quarterly reviews are generally recommended to promote and enhance learning among children.

Thus assessment may be on:

- *Daily basis:* Interacting with students and continuously assessing them both in situations inside and outside the classroom.
- *Periodic*: Once in every 3 to 4 weeks, teachers may check and reflect on the information collected. This however should not be in the form of a test or exam.

Methods of Assessment

Before choosing any method, it is necessary to decide the kind of arrangement that is best suited for the type of information needed. There are four basic methods of organizing assessments, namely:

- *Individual Assessment*: which focuses on one student while she/he is doing an activity or task and thus recognises individual work and accomplishments.
- *Group Assessment*: which focuses on the learning and progress of a group of students working on a task together with the objective of completing it. This method of organization is found to be more useful in order to assess social skills, co-operative learning processes and other value related dimensions of a student's behaviour.
- *Self-Assessment:* refers to the student's own assessment of her/his learning and progress in knowledge, skills, processes, interests, attitudes etc.

- *Peer-Assessment:* refers to one student assessing other children. This can be conducted in pairs or in groups.

Assessment can become a useful and interesting process. To realize this you need to be careful about:

- Being clear about why you are assessing the student.
- Not labelling students as slow, poor, intelligent, dull or making comparisons between students.
- Using a variety of ways to collect information about the student's learning and progress in subjects and across curricular boundaries.
- Collecting information continuously and recording the same.
- Giving importance to each student's way of responding and learning and the time it takes to do so.
- Reporting on ongoing, continuous basis and being sensitive to every student's responses.
- Not making negative statements, or using technical language during assessment, or while providing feedback to the student, parents or others.
- Providing feedback in clear and simple language which will lead to positive action and help the student to do better.

Inclusive Classroom

To make inclusive education possible, to accommodate students with different learning abilities, the present education system and educational practices need to become more flexible, more inclusive and more collaborative.

A school can deal with the differently-abled students by forming teams consisting of the school counsellor, class teacher, peer mentor or buddy.

Assessing Co-Scholastic Areas

All teachers need to be involved in Assessing Co-Scholastic Skills of children for the following reasons:

(*a.*) Reduces Subjectivity

(*b.*) Removes Bias

(*c.*) Provides a point of reference to all teachers

(*d.*) Makes all teachers involved and accountable

(*e.*) Distributes work load amongst teachers

(*f.*) Simplifies work with regularly maintained record, on computer

Empowerment of Teachers

No educational scheme can succeed unless the teachers are adequately prepared for executing it and have faith in its worth. This preparation will resume the visualization of a realistic scheme and the development of comprehensive procedures for its operational implementation. Teachers need to be provided orientation about the scheme. For providing orientation trained resource persons need to be created.

The content of such training and orientation programmes, has to incorporate both the Scholastic and Co-Scholastic Areas of learners' growth. The development of improved evaluation tools and their appropriate use, is an important aspect of these courses. With respect to the Scholastic Areas, it would require the preparation of objective based questions, balanced question papers, scoring of scripts, analysis and declaration of results. Regarding the Co-Scholastic Areas, it would mean the preparation and use of rating scales, inventories, checklists, schedules and the procedures of assessing different areas of skills. Training in the methods of collecting, recording, compiling and interpreting evidences of learners growth will be other crucial aspects of these training programmes.

5

Achievement Tests

Achievement tests are tests of developed skill or knowledge. The most common type of achievement test is a standardized test developed to measure skills and knowledge learned in a given grade level, usually through planned instruction, such as training or classroom instruction. Achievement tests are often contrasted with tests that measure aptitude, a more general and stable cognitive trait.

Achievement test scores are often used in an educational system to determine what level of instruction for which a student is prepared. High achievement scores usually indicate a mastery of grade-level material, and the readiness for advanced instruction. Low achievement scores can indicate the need for remediation or repeating a course grade.

When writing achievement test items, writers usually begin with a list of content standards (either written by content specialists or based on state-created content standards) which specify exactly what students are expected to learn in a given school year. The goal of item writers is to create test items that measure the most important skills and knowledge attained in a given grade-level. The number and type of test items written is determined by the grade-level content standards. Content validity is determined by the representativeness of the items included on the final test.

PURPOSE OF ACHIEVEMENT TESTS

Achievement tests are universally used in the classroom mainly for the following purposes:

1. To measure whether students possess the prerequisite skills needed to succeed in any unit or whether the students have achieved the objective of the planned instruction.
2. To monitor students' learning and to provide ongoing feedback to both students and teachers during the teaching-learning process.
3. To identify the students' learning difficulties—whether persistent or recurring.
4. To assign grades.

Construction of Achievement Tests

There are several steps involved in the construction of Achievement Tests. We will now discuss these in detail one by one.

Instructional Objectives

The first and the most important step in planning a test is to identify the instructional objectives. Each subject has a different set of instructional objectives. In the subjects of Science, Social Sciences, and Mathematics the major objectives are categorized as knowledge, understanding, application and skill, while in Languages the major objectives are categorized as knowledge, comprehension and expression. Knowledge objective is considered to be the lowest level of learning whereas understanding, application of knowledge in sciences or behavioural sciences are considered higher levels of learning.

Design

The second step in planning a test is to make the "Design". The Design specifies weightages to different *(a)* instructional objectives, *(b)* types (or forms) of questions, *(c)* units and sub-units of the course content, *(d)* levels of difficulty. It also indicates as to whether there are any options in the question paper, and if so, what their nature is?

The Design, in fact, is termed as an instrument which reflects major policy decisions of the examining agency, whether it is a Board or an individual.

Blueprint

The third step is to prepare the "Blueprint". The policy decisions, as reflected in the design of the question paper, are translated into action through the Blueprint. It is at this stage that the paper setter decides as to how many question are to be set for different objectives. Further he/she decides under which unit/topic a particular question is to be set. Furthermore, he/she picks up various forms of questions. Thereafter, the paper setter decides how all the questions are to be distributed over different objectives and content areas so as to obtain the weightages decided in the Design. The three dimensions of the blueprint consist of content areas in horizontal rows and objectives and forms of questions in vertical columns. Once the blueprint is prepared, the paper setter can write/select the items and prepare the question paper.

Writing of Questions

The next step after the finalization of the blueprint is writing appropriate questions in accordance with the broad parameters set out in the blueprint. One should take one small block of the blueprint at a time and write out the required questions. Thus, for each block of blueprint which is filled in, questions have got to be written one by one. Once it is done, we have all the questions meeting the necessary requirements laid down in the blueprint. While selecting each small block for writing a question, you can proceed in several ways.

(*a*) either writing all questions (one by one) belonging to one objective at a time i.e. knowledge or understanding or application followed by other objectives, or

(*b*) by taking up questions according to their form or type i.e. Essay Type followed by Short Answer and Very Short Answer Type or in any other order, or

(*c*) by writing questions for one unit of the syllabus or portion to be covered by the test at a time.

Each approach has its advantages and disadvantages, too. Irrespective of the method followed, the questions then have to be arranged in a logical sequence.

Marking Scheme

The fifth step is to prepare the "Marking Scheme". The marking scheme helps prevent inconsistency in judgement. In the marking scheme, possible responses to items in the test are structured. The various value points for response are graded and the marks allowed to each value point indicated. The marking scheme ensures objectivity in judgement and eliminates differences in score which may be due to idiosyncrasies of the evaluator. The marking scheme, of course^ includes the scoring key, which is prepared in respect of objective type questions.

Apart from the quality of the question paper, reliability of assessment, to a great extent, depends on the degree of consistency of scores assigned to the students by different examiners or by the same examiner on two different occassions. Thus, variation can occur because of any one of two different reasons:

(*i*) Due to inconsistency of the same examiner when he/she examines different answer scripts adopting different standards.

(*ii*) Due to different examiners using different standards of judgement.

If an answer script is awarded the same grade or marks on repeated exposure to the same examiner, the examiner is said to be consistent in awarding the marks. As such, the assessment done by him/her could be said to be more reliable and consistent than the other examiner in whose case variation in award of marks is higher.

The factor contributing to variations in the standards of assessment, both at the intra-and the inter-examiner levels, can be controlled by supplying a detailed scheme of marking along with the expected answers so that every examiner may interpret the questions in the same way and attain the same standard of marking without being too lenient or strict or varying in his/her assessment. Subjectivity, is thus minimised and it is believed to give a more reliable picture of the students' performance.

Highlights of a good marking scheme

1. It is a three column statement showing serial number of the questions, their expected outline answers and the marks allotted to each value point under them.
2. In respect of long answer or essay type questions, the expected outline answers should:

   (*i*) be complete and cover all possible or major areas as demanded by the questions (*ii*) clearly indicate each expected point or the parts under the outlined major areas

(*iii*) provide direction as to whether all points will count towards a complete or correct answer or a set of points will be adequate enough for full credit (All this should be clearly reflected), and

(*iv*) indicate marks for each expected point Marks so distributed over expected points or their sets should be equal to the total marks assigned for a question.

3. In respect of short answer questions a complete answer may be provided with its break-ups where ever necessary along with the break-up of marks.
4. Out of the total marks assigned for a question, each point so enumerated/explained may be assigned marks according to their significance in the answer.
5. In some situations, apart from the content, other qualities of answer may also matter significantly, particularly in long answer or essay type questions. These could be logical approach, coherence, lucidity of expression, the style of presentation etc. Some marks may also be set apart for such overall quality of answer which cannot be usually covered in enumeration of the content points.
6. The scheme of marking needs to be comprehensive enough not to leave any point unexpected and thus should provide clear guidelines in respect of the break-up of marks over different points or parts of the answer.
7. If a question entails some other points beyond one's expectation, a provision may also be made to take them into account and suitably reward them.

Question-wise Analysis

The sixth and the last step is that of question-wise

analysis. Such an exercise helps the paper setter to ensure that there is no imbalance in the question paper. During question-wise analysis, the paper setter analyses each question on various parameters stated in the blueprint.

ADMINISTRATION OF AN ACHIEVEMENT TEST

Having prepared a good test, you should plan to administer it in such a way that each of your students will do his/her best.

Motivating students is very important, and this is an area in which each teacher will have his/her own special technique. If you can get your students to see this test as an interesting and challenging task, which will benefit them, they will surely do well. Let them understand the advantages of the class test. Make them understand that such tests help them to get a feedback on their weaknesses and misunderstandings, which can be corrected before they face external examinations. Experience has shown that students who are given frequent class tests and are subjected to continuous assessment do better in external examinations.

Some of the values of designing a good test and preparing students well for the test may be lost if you do not plan in advance for its administration. Detailed planning is necessary as any confusion in the administration of a test is found to disturb the examinee and lower the validity of the results. Some tips to be kept in mind while planning for the administration of a lest are given below:

Time Schedule

Be sure you plan your time schedule carefully, ensuring teacher and pupil readiness. Much preparation may be done a day before. It will be wise to schedule enough time for briefing the invigilators.

If there is a deadline for finishing and leaving the room (e.g., the end of a class period), be specially sure to plan for adequate time at the end for the things which must be done. Even with a small class these take five to ten minutes, and with a large group they may take at least fifteen minutes. A hasty wind-up may result in non-fulfilment of the objectives of the test, or other disasters.

The Room

It is important for any examination to provide a quite, comfortable atmosphere, in which the students are encouraged to do their best. As much as possible, try to test in a quiet place with a minimum of distracting noises. Avoid rooms near cafeterias, important hallways, playing fields or other noisy places. Request nearby loudspeaker owners to shut them off for the duration of the examination hours. Hang signs on the door, saying "EXAMINATION IN PROGRESS: DO NOT DISTURB". Objective examinations generally require more intense concentration than essay type exams. The latter demand an excess of physical endurance. Objective tests require constant, careful and critical thinking and reasoning, with a minimum of physical work.

Desks, Etc.

Remembjer that the students will be writing on a single—thickness answer sheet, not a thick answer book. Be sure the writing surfaces are at least 30 x 38 cm., and as smooth as possible. If there are cracks or scratches a student's pencil may push through the answer sheet, spoiling it and making it hard to mark. Also be sure the room is clear of any charts, posters, etc. that might help some candidates.

Equipment

It is wise to make up a check-list, ahead of time, of what

you will have to take with you to the examination hall. Be sure to include chalk to write necessary notices on the black board. If there is no black board make up placards or poster ahead of time. Also invest in a dozen or so soft pencils, preferably with erasers. This is in case some students (*a*) bring hard pencils, or (*b*) break a pencil and don't have a spare pencil. For exact timing of the test (much more important for objective tests) it is better to have two watches or clocks, in case one stops.

Invigilators

For anything more than an informal, half-period quiz, you will probably need the help of one or more invigilators. Chose persons who are willing to give their full attention to the task. Neither you nor your invigilators should talk, read, correct papers or do any other work during the examination time. They should observe closely, circulating constantly, checking that the students are answering in the right place, using soft pencils, not copying etc. However, they should riot hover too long over any student, as this makes the examinee nervous.

SCORING AND RECORDING OF TEST RESULTS

Despite the objectivity of scoring short answer tests, certain procedures are indispensable if scoring is to be done with maximum accuracy and efficiency. The necessity for extreme care in scoring has been indicated by several studies showing that scoring errors occur with appalling frequency. "Constant'.' errors can be due to failure to understand scoring directions, with resultant scores which are consistently too low or too high. "Variable" errors can be due to carelessness in marking, adding, computing, or transcribing scores. These errors warrant (1) the careful training and instruction of scorers and (2) the rescoring of at least a sample of any group of test booklets or answer sheets.

Order of Scoring

With essay tests it may be desirable to have one person score all answers to the first question, then to the second, and so on. If, for objective tests separate answer sheets are provided, the scorer may score a given page in all booklets first, then the next page, and so on, rather than scoring all of one booklet before going on to the next. If so many booklets must be scored that several scorers are needed, each person may specialize on a given page or group of pages of the booklet but should score only one page in all booklets at a time.

Rescoring

With a large number of booklets to be scored and sufficient help available, it is always worthwhile to rescore them so as to eliminate errors that otherwise are almost inevitable in a clerical task like this. If complete rescoring is not feasible every fifth or tenth booklet should be rescored to get a rough idea of the frequency and magnitude of scoring errors. Rescoring a sample sometimes uncovers such an inaccuracy as to make it desirable to rescore the remainder.

Keeping Records

As soon as possible after the tests have been administered, the answer sheet should be checked and scared, and the scores should be recorded on the permanent records of the school. Each teacher; should be given copies of the score reports for the pupils in his/her classes. Usually schools have some type of permanent record for each pupil which provides space for recording standardized test results.

The form in which test results are recorded is often meaningless to anyone except the persons recording them. Sometimes permanent records for a student contain such information as the following:

IQ	104	Mathematics	97
Reading	68	Science	93

What do these scores mean? What test of intelligence was used ? What was its standard deviation? Are the Reading, Mathematics and Science scores the raw scores, percentile ranks, or same other type of standard or derived score? Unless the cumulative record contains complete information about the test and the type of score, the effort involved in carrying on a testing program, scoring the tests, and reporting the scores is practically wasted. If the records are to have value, the following must be indicated: test title, form of the test, dale when the test was given, the raw score or standard score, and percentile rank under properly identified captions. When percentile ranks are reported, the group on which the norms were based should be identified—for example, national, state, district, local, or other group—and the nature of the group should be specified.

NORMS AND INTERPRETATION OF TEST SCORES

Norms are based on frequency distributions and in general, half of any group of pupils falls below its average and half above it. A norm is not the "ideal performance" of a group of pupils; it is only the typical performance of typical students at a given time. Hence educators should avoid the fallacy of insisting on bringing everyone up to the norm. School practices resulting from attempts to get all pupils to be like the "average" have held back many superior students and created emotional problems among the less able. Such practices have caused much criticism of education through the years. Benjamin Franklin is reported to have said that "the schools are polishing the bricks and dulling the diamonds."

Local Factors

Many local factors should be taken into account when interpreting the standing of pupils according to norms derived on a nationwide basis. Among these factors are (1) the legal age for entering school, (2) the average age of actually entering school, (3) promotion and detention policies, (4) rate and selectivity of elimination from school, (5) efficiency of the teaching personnel, (6) the grade placement and time allowances, (7) general nature of the curriculum, (8) the standing of local pupils in mental ability and other aspects related to the one being evaluated, (9) the relative emphasis in the local school on academic, social, and vocational development, and (10) the home background of pupils. The meaning of the derived scores for a given group of students can then be interpreted in the light of these factors.

When interpreting the performance of individual students or of a class as a whole, the teacher should take into special consideration differences in the cultural background of families and communities. There are wide variations in the kind of experiences students have. We can expect that differences in language background, richness of home resources, and intensity of the desire for an education will be reflected in student performance.

Performance of students also varies with varying emphasis on different aspects of the school curriculum. In some subject matter areas, such as Arithmetic, the teacher usually cannot expect his/her students to go much beyond instructional materials. In other areas such as reading, there are many opportunities for students to develop skill and knowledge on their own outside the school programme. Thus the performance of individuals and groups should be judged, in part at least, on the basis of the curriculum to which they have been exposed. When the performance of a class or an individual deviates considerably from the norms on standardized tests, a need for reappraisal of the school curriculum and of teaching emphases may be indicated. In many practical situations it is necessary to use norms whose applicability to local conditions is questionable or unknown. To the extent that it is so, the data obtained from them cannot be interpreted meaningfully for individual students.

A final precaution is to avoid using tests to punish pupils or to foster a spirit of rivalry among teachers or schools. Teachers and administrators must keep the welfare of students uppermost in their minds and be sensitive to the requirements of adequate human relations. Failure to do this in administering and interpreting a testing programme has produced negative feelings about tests in both pupils and teachers. So much for qualitative interpretations.

GRADES

What is grading? In the system of grading, students are classified into a few ability groups or categories according to their level of achievement in an examination. The achievement is defined in the form of numerical or letter grades, each of which denotes a certain level of performance, generally not in absolute terms but in relation to the performance of the whole group.

Grading is essentially meant for categorizing students into a few ability groups on the basis of their performance in the examination. There are two approaches to formation of groups that define the grades *(a)* on the basis of absolute marks and *(b)* on the basis of relative marks or rank order of marks. Let us see what these mean and also consider their merits and demerits.

Absolute Grading

This approach involves direct conversion of marks into

grades. Whatever be the distribution of marks in a subject, the marks between two fixed points on 0-100 scale would correspond to a given grade. An example of this is the categorisation of students into 5 groups—Distinction, 1st, 2nd, 3rd Division and fail categories on the basis of marks as follows:

75 or above	Distinction
60-74	1st Division
45-59	2nd Division
33-44	3rd Division
Below 33	Fail

It is possible to form any number of groups to correspond to grades (A,B,C etc.) in this way on the basis of marks. However, in view of the disparity in the distribution of marks of different subjects, Grade A of one subject cannot be treated at par with Grade A of another subject though Grade A is based on the same cutoff point in both the subjects. For example, if it is decided to award Grade A to those scoring 90 per cent or more whatever be the subject, there may be no student getting Grade A in English or History while quite a few will be getting grade A in Mathematics. In a sense it only serves as a substitute for individual marking system except that it gives a number of ability groups.

Comparative Grading

This involves conversion of marks into grades on the basis of rank order or percentiles. In this case the distribution of marks is taken into consideration while determining the range of marks corresponding to different grades. For example, the top 5 per cent students may be given grade A, the next 10 per cent grade B and so on. Here the actual cut-off score for grade A in one subject may be quite different from that of another subject. In this case the grade that a student gels depends on his/her relative performance, that is, on what his/her marks are in relation to the marks of others.

Advantages

In general when we talk of grading it is only the type of grading based on relative marks that we have in mind. These grades are expressed in the form of letters A, B, C etc. The following are the main advantages of such grading:

(i) With the same uniform pattern being adopted for all subjects, grading would provide better comparability of the results of different years in the same subject.

(ii) Grading is essentially based on rank ordering of students. Studies have shown that agreement among examiners on ranks to be awarded to examinees is much more in this than on absolute marks. Hence grades based on rank order in general, are more reliable.

(iii) There is greater comparability among subjects when grades are used. When there is a choice of subjects, students need not avoid the subjects which are considered low scoring. Even with a so called low scoring subject, the proportion of students getting a grade would be nearly the same as in a so called high scoring subject

(iv) Grades in different subjects in an examination provide a meaningful profile of the achievement of a student. Unlike marks, one can easily find out in which subjects the performance is outstanding, good, fair or poor. With marks, one can arrive at such inference only on knowing what the range, average and dispersion are of the marks in the different subjects.

6

Diagnostics Tests

Diagnostic testing is an important tool for educators who want to know where their students are academically in order to bring those students to where they need to be. If you want your students to move forward, you need to identify where they have started; diagnostic testing is the way to do this.

A diagnostic test measures where a student is in terms of his knowledge and skills. It will assess the abilities that student has at a particular time to solve problems or answer questions in a subject area. Teachers use diagnostic tests to assess students' strengths and weaknesses in her subject area. It shows how much they know about the subject and also how much more they still need to know before they leave the class.

Diagnostic tests can be especially beneficial for teachers who have multiple classes to teach within one subject. A diagnostic test given to all classes can show that teacher, for example, that 1st period students are comfortable with fractions but 3rd period students still need some practice in that area.

A diagnostic test is useful if a teacher uses it more than once throughout the school year. Given at the beginning of the year it can help him plan his instruction.

Midyear he can determine how much students have learned so far and what he needs to re-teach. At the end of the year it can provide an assessment of a student's total learning for the class.

IMPORTANCE OF EDUCATIONAL DIAGNOSIS

The term educational diagnosis includes all activities in measurement and interpretation that help to "identify growth" and their causal factors for individuals or for class groups. Diagnosis in education resembles diagnosis in medicine. The aids used most frequently for diagnosis are known as diagnostic tests. These tests are used to obtain a picture of pupil difficulties. The process of determining the causes of educational difficulties is known as educational diagnosis.

Educational diagnosis implies the use of technical procedures designed to locate specific learning and instructional difficulties, and if possible, to determine their causes. For the medical expert, diagnosis means the careful and extensive observation of the patient under controlled conditions. It includes the use of professional instruments, such as the clinical thermometer, the stethoscope, and the microscope, which make possible exact and objective observation. It means the assembly of a complete case history of the background of the difficulty, the examination and analysis of many similar cases, in order that common factors may be identified.

Unfortunately, much of the exactness, objectivity, and precision of the medical diagnostician's instruments are likely to be missing in the teacher's equipment. Even today only a few objective measuring instruments capable of rendering reasonably precise diagnosis are available to the pedagogical diagnostician. The well prepared modern teacher now has at hand reasonably adequate statistical techniques, analytical diagnostic tests in different subjects and diagnostic charts. They also have instruments and devices for measuring oral activity, vision, and binocular fusion and many other highly important qualities that may account for a pupil's lack of progress in many fields of learning. It is thus apparent that diagnosis in education is moving rapidly in the direction of scientific accuracy.

The diagnosis of difficulties underlying educational accomplishment undoubtedly constitutes the high point in the supervisory and instructional uses of educational tests.

Deficiencies of a general nature are revealed and brought to light by general survey tests. Specific weaknesses, and to a certain extent the causes of such weaknesses, are identified by the use of properly selected diagnostic tests. Practically all of the more exact types of diagnostic procedures, such as the location of defects in speech, hearing, and vision, are dependent upon educational test results for their initial steps.

ANALYSIS AS THE BASIS OF DIAGNOSIS

The successful development of school learning depends upon the care with which the underlying and basic skills of the subjects themselves are recognised and utilized in teaching. For instance, teaching a child to add consists not only in developing the habit of responding automatically and correctly to the basic combinations but also involves higher levels of skill, such as bridging of the tens, control of the attention span, and carrying from one column to the next. The teacher's task is made obvious and objective if he/she understands this. Similarly, it can be shown that silent reading comprehension is not a single isolated ability. It is a composite of many elements, such as knowledge of word meanings, ability to get meaning from sentences, ability to arrange through unit and sentence units into logically organized wholes, and ability to find desired material quickly. The teacher has a real basis for instructional procedures with this knowledge.

Language is another basic subject in which many delicately balanced skills are interwoven in an extremely complex manner. Here again the elements of achievement in the total process must be identified. Blind trust in general practice on the total skill must necessarily give way to the exact identification and discovery of the particular points of pupil weakness as a basis for special emphasis.

Good diagnosis must parallel the process of good teaching. Effective diagnostic materials in any school subject can be prepared only after the skills contributing to success in that subject have been isolated and identified. Psychologically, the reason for this is that on the whole the child learns to do what he/she practices or does. Remedial work, accordingly, can function only when the point at which pupil mastery breaks down has been located. Thus, the analysis must be penetrating and the diagnosis must be precise.

SPECIFIC NATURE OF DIAGNOSIS

Diagnosis must be more exact than merely a broad statement of general functions. It is not enough to discover that a child is unable to read silently. The exact nature of his/her handicap must be revealed before it is possible to undertake a remedial programme. The more specific the diagnostic information revealed, the more exactly the remedial material can be made to fit the need. To return to a frequently used illustration, if it is found by diagnosis that a child is unable to add, unless the exact point at which his/her mastery of addition breaks down can be determined by the diagnosis, teaching or remedial efforts are largely wasted. One of the outstanding reasons why more effective teaching and remedial work has not been done in certain fields is that no adequate analysis of basic skills can be made or has been made.

Diagnostic Use of Test Results

Tests as such are incapable of improving instruction because of any inherent power. Existing conditions are merely revealed by them. Remedial or corrective teaching is the result of deliberated constructive effort by the teacher after the particular points of weakness in the instruction of the pupils have been revealed by the tests. The ease, clearness, and directness with which these needs are revealed by the tests are a measure of their real educational value. Very few existing tests are so constructed as to permit the interpretation of their results directly in terms of an effective remedial procedure. However, this seems to be no good reason for the failure of teachers to apply more directly the results of this work in testing to the improvement of their teaching practice. Just as the data revealed by the navigator's instruments require calculation and interpretation, so is it necessary to analyse test data carefully in order to make them the basis of genuine remedial programme.

The interpretation of test scores and the planning of remedial procedures are the most difficult and also the most important parts of the use of educational test results. One of the greatest needs in education today is the provision for genuine diagnostic testing in all instructional fields, supplemented by valid remedial work designed to correct the weaknesses and defects of individual pupils as revealed by the tests. It is important to learn, as a result of using tests in the classroom, that a pupil or the entire class is below the norm in the subject, but unless it is learned with some exactness what causes the low level of achievement, the testing programme will do little, if anything, more than supply interesting information.

Diagnosis as the Basis for Remedial Work

Accurate diagnosis of class and individual pupil difficulties, coupled with application of remedy is not only important but necessary for teachers. The success of the remedial or corrective teaching depends upon the accuracy and detail with which the specific skills involved in successful achievement in the subject are identified and isolated in the test. Tests of the general survey type, or tests that report single unanalyzed scores, cannot supply this information in sufficient detail.

Diagnosis as the Basis for Preventive Work

An examination of the number and types of skills identified as a result of the diagnostic methods discussed in the preceding section leads to a suggestion of a still more constructive use of analytic and diagnostic test results. Diagnosis as applied in education has taken on a meaning indicative of a breakdown in method, a failure of instructional techniques. Unquestionably, one of the basic purposes of diagnosis is the location of weaknesses and the determination of their causes, but there is nothing in the method that precludes its use in the prevention of weaknesses through anticipation of their causes. Out of the knowledge gained through the use of diagnostic procedures should come the basis for preventive work of all types. It is quite noticeable that the major emphasis in the fields of dentistry and medicine is not on correction but on prevention. The existence of a weakness implies a failure at some point in the programme. The discovery of it would not be marked as important merely because it is then possible to correct it The real importance in the discovery should lie rather in the prevention of its reappearance elsewhere under similar conditions.

Another illustration from the field of medicine may make this point somewhat more concrete. In every medical examination for diagnostic purposes a complete analysis is made and an exact case record of all observations is kept. Out of the analysis of these records has come a better understanding of the causes and characteristics of certain types of human ailments. Out of this same type of analysis has also come the basis for much of the preventive work that characterizes modern medical science.

In a similar way, accurate and detailed educational diagnosis may ultimately offer the basis for the development of a program of preventive work in education. For example, if after diagnosing the addition of fractions in the fifth grade, it is found that the failure of pupils to reduce the fractions to their lowest terms in the answers is a common weakness, the obvious thing to do is to correct the defects at once and then proceed to reconstruct the first instruction so that the following year the causes for this particular weakness may not operate so powerfully. Similarly, any weakness identified now should afford the basis for decisions calculated to reduce the probability of their recurrence in the future.

DIAGNOSTIC TESTS: PURPOSE AND USE

Diagnostic tests are designed to point out inadequacies in specific skills. The immediate aim is to locate areas in which additional instruction is required or in which teaching methods have to be improved. The purpose of diagnostic testing is to furnish continuous specific information in order that learning activities may be most productive of desirable outcomes. Diagnostic tests would be helpful in identifying the use of faulty, round-about or incorrect procedures; the use of elementary processes where these could have been replaced by advanced processes; and evidences of lack of understanding and lack of precision. A carefully constructed test could be used as an inventory test towards the beginning of a year's work or topic and as analytical test of competencies or skills involved in the different branches or units of study.

The diagnostic test results will reveal in a comprehensive way, the exact level reached by students and the precise nature of the difficulties. These tests will help to find out the specific kind of instruction and practice that will be required to bring achievement upto the desired level. To tackle large classes, individual observation needs to be supplemented through diagnostic tests. The tests are useful as guides to both the attainments as well as difficulties of students whose achievements are not up to the mark; in isolating individual difficulties; and for dividing students into groups for special coaching or remedial teaching as the case may be.

DIAGNOSTIC EVALUATION VS. SUMMATIVE AND FORMATIVE EVALUATION

Diagnostic evaluation is concerned with the pupils' persistent or recurring learning difficulties that are left unresolved during the course of classroom teaching and formative evaluation. If a pupil continues to experience failure in Reading, Mathematics, or other subjects, despite the use of prescribed alternate methods of instruction (e.g. programmed materials, visual aids) then the need for a more detailed diagnosis is indicated. To use a medical analogy, formative evaluation provides first-aid treatment for simple learning problems, and diagnostic evaluation searches for the underlying causes of those problems that do not respond to first-aid treatment. Thus, diagnostic evaluation is much more comprehensive and detailed. It involves the use of specially prepared diagnostic tests as well as various observational techniques. Serious learning problems are also likey to require the services of psychologists, and medical specialists. The primary aim of diagnostic evaluation is to determine the causes of learning problems and to formulate a plan for remedial action.

The difference between diagnostic evaluation and such types as summative and formative evaluation is perhaps best reflected in the sort of answers each type is expected to elicit and the uses typically made of the evaluation results.

With summative evaluation, the central question is: How well has the student achieved the learning objectives by the end of a period of study, that is, by the end of a textbook chapter or by the end of the school year? Results are typically used for grading or certifying students, judging the effectiveness of the teacher, and sometimes evaluating the curriculum.

With formative evaluation, the question is: During a period of study, how well is the student progressing towards mastering the various learning objectives ? The results are typically used for giving the students and teachers feedback on the students' progress and consequently, for locating errors in terms of the structure of a study so that remedial alternative instruction techniques can be adopted.

ACHIEVEMENT TESTS VS. DIAGNOSTIC TESTS

Achievement tests are used to measure the relative accomplishment of students in specified areas of learning. From the point of view of diagnosis, the total score on an achievement test is not of any valuable help.

Achievement test results reveal difficulties only when they are originally designed for diagnostic purposes. The diagnostic test differs from an ordinary classroom test or a standardized achievement test in that its main object is to analyse and not to assess. In a diagnostic test, the speed factor is neglected and ample time is provided for pupils to complete as much of the task as they can.

The two differ in scope and nature of coverage. Diagnostic tests are generally designed for students of below average performance in the particular subject(s). On the other hand achievement tests are, in theory, meant for the average students. The diagnostic tests are meant to identify difficulties and weaknesses so that these can be remedied while achievement tests are aimed at evaluating the achievement level of students in order to grade them and compare them with other students. The diagnostic tests concentrate on the areas of perceived difficulty as observed during the teaching-learning process, while achievement tests have to cover the whole unit learnt. As far as the analysis of answers is concerned, achievement tests are checked and marked for finding out what and how much has been learnt while diagnostic tests are used to find out what has not been learnt and to locate the exact source of the difficulty ? A diagnostic test is an evaluative procedure which stresses incidental rather than crucial objectives that are determined before hand for guiding educational activity. The test attempts to identify those specific elements which may hinder learning and adjustment. An ideal diagnostic test should contain a cross-section of the test items that reflect the various aspects of achievement which the student should possess.

DIAGNOSIS AND REMEDIATION OF LEARNING DIFFICULTIES

There are four major steps in the diagnosis and

remediation of learning difficulties: (1) Determining which students are having learning difficulty, (2) Determining the specific nature of the learning difficulty, (3) Determining the factors causing the learning difficulty, (4) Application of appropriate remedial procedures. Testing and evaluation can make a significant contribution to each of these steps.

Determining who is having Difficulty

There are a number of methods for identifying those pupils who are experiencing learning difficulty. One of the most common is to observe/analyse the results of achievement tests.

In some cases it is desirable to analyze an achievement test item by item and make a tally of those missed by each student. Items which are missed by a large number of students indicate areas where the class as a whole is doing poorly. This might suggest that either the test has inadequate content validity, or that changes in teaching method are needed. The errors of each individual student can also be studied for clues to his/her particular learning difficulties.

A major caution in using an analysis of item responses to determine individual learning difficulties pertains to the small number of items representing each area. At best, such an analysis merely provides clues which must be followed up by further study and observation.

Informal classroom evaluation procedures can also be used to detect learning difficulties. Anecdotal records, and other observational devices provide clues to identifying learning problems. The day-to-day observations and judgements of an experienced teacher are especially valuable; he/she frequently can spot a student's difficulty before it becomes serious.

In determining which pupils are having learning difficulty, we should not confine our efforts to those with problems in the basic skills and the content areas. Students who are having difficulty in social relations, emotional adjustment, and other aspects of personal-social development also require attention. Learning problems of this type are significant in their own right, and they have a direct bearing on the student's ability to learn in other areas.

Determining the Specific Nature of Learning Difficulties

The diagnosis of learning difficulties is a matter of degree. In some instances, the general procedures for locating pupils with learning difficulties provide sufficient information for immediate corrective action. In other cases, it may be necessary to supplement this information by further diagnostic study before planning remedial work. In still others, the learning problem may be so persistent and severe that the student should be referred to a specialist for intensive diagnosis.

When a student's learning difficulty is in one of the basic areas, a logical follow-up procedure is the administration of a diagnostic test. Such tests are based on the common errors pupils make and thus provide a systematic method for locating the specific problem. Diagnostic tests tend to provide a more reliable sample of a student's errors than general achievement tests because they have a large number of items representing each particular aspect of the skill being measured. The test manuals and accessory materials accompanying published diagnostic tests typically provide suggestions for further diagnosis and for use of the test scores in remedial work.

The procedure of analyzing a student's responses to each test item, described in the previous section, is one approach to this problem. Another is to administer a general achievement lest and ask the students to describe aloud the mental process they are following as they answer each question. The "thinking aloud" provides clues to the student's weaknesses in knowledge, skill " and method of approaching problems. Since the test is administered on an individual basis, it is also possible to note any emotional factors or undesirable habits which might be interfering with the student's responses. Clues concerning the specific nature of a student's learning difficulties might also be inferred from his/her cumulative record. An.examination of past results, course grades, anecdotal records, and other evaluative data can frequently throw light on the nature of a pupil's present difficulty. This, of course, is also a vital step in searching for the causes of the problem.

Determining the Factors Causing Learning Difficulty

Some learning difficulties can be attributed to improper teaching methods, unsuitable curricular emphasis, or exceptionally complex course materials. Evaluation results can contribute to improved instruction.

Of particular interest to us here are the persistent learning difficulties of individual pupils that cannot be accounted for by formal instruction. To determine the causes of these problems we must make a careful study of the pupil and his/her environment. The major areas to consider are work-study skills; health and physical condition; emotional adjustment and home environment. unfavourable factors in any of these areas cause or contribute to learning problems.

It should be noted that the causes of learning difficulties are multiple and complex and can seldom be fully determined by the classroom teacher. However, a review of the student's cumulative record, special testing and observations (as needed), an interview with the pupil, and possibly a home visit, should provide sufficient information on which to base remedial action. If the student's learning problem requires more extended study than can be accomplished within the normal teaching situation, the pupil should be referred to a specialist.

Applying Remedial Procedures

There is no set pattern to be followed for helping pupils overcome learning difficulties. In some instances it may be a simple matter of review and re-touching. In others, an extensive effort to improve motivation, correct emotional difficulties, and overcome deficiencies in work-study skills may be required. The specific remedial procedures used in any given case will depend on the specific nature of the learning difficulty and the factors which have caused and contributed to it.

Testing and evaluation can play a vital role in most remedial programs. The use of periodic testing during remedial teaching might serve the following functions; (1) clarify to the pupils the specific types of responses that are expected; (2) provide further diagnostic information about the pupils' difficulties and learning needs; (3) give the pupils a feeling of success through the use of a carefully graded series of test exercises; (4) enhance motivation by providing short-term goals and immediate knowledge of progress; and (5) provide information concerning the effectiveness of the remedial procedures.

Though the immediate aim of remedial work is the correction of specific learning difficulties, our interest should not stop there. A careful analysis of evaluation results during diagnosis and treatment will reveal learning errors that can be prevented and causal factors that can be modified. The ultimate result of a remedial program should be more effective instructional methods.

In summary, evaluation procedures are useful in all phases of diagnostic and remedial work. Although they serve essentially the same functions here as for the general instructional programme, attention in diagnosis is focused more directly on the specific responses of individual pupils.

DIAGNOSTIC TESTING

Diagnosis of persistent learning difficulties involves much more than diagnostic testing, but such tests are useful in the total process. The diagnostic test takes up where the formative test leaves off. If pupils do not respond to the feedback-corrective prescriptions of formative testing they need for & more detailed search for the source of learning errors is indicated. Such tests are also commonly called learning tests, quizzes, unit tests, and the like. We will need to include a number of test items in each specific area with some slight variation from item to item. While diagnosing pupil's difficulties in adding whole numbers, for example, we would want to include addition problems containing various number combinations with some not requiring carrying and some requiring carrying, to pinpoint the specific types of error each students is making. Since our focus is on the pupils' learning difficulties, diagnostic tests must be constructed in light of the most common sources of error encountered by students. Such tests are typically confined to a limited area of instruction, and the test item tends to have a relatively low level of difficulty.

The Teacher and Diagnostic Testing

Diagnosis is an important factor in imparting instruction.

Instruction will not be complete without diagnosis and remedial teaching, individuals differ and in a class of forty or fifty, pupils of different levels of ability are likely to be present. Naturally, there will be slow learners and fast learners as also average learners. They have to be catered to in different ways or at least a balance has to be maintained.

Tests are a must in schools and they in turn yield sufficient data to guide the child in addition to reporting attainment. The answer papers, if analysed, will provide useful data on the weaknesses of students. It is all the more true in the case of terminal and annual examination papers. Even the answer scripts of test papers will give clues to the types of mistakes that a child is likely to commit. An error analysis has to be attempted in order to diagnose the difficulties. If tests are administered towards the end of sub-topics, the analysis of the papers will yield more information than on a composite test.

A test has to be devised with enough number of items to represent all possible types of mistakes. Repetition of situations is important in any diagnostic test. The different types of questions are best suited for certain purposes, hence the type of tests included is also a contributing factor to the success of the test. Clarity and specificity of items included and their preciseness are to be judged in evaluating diagnostic tests prepared by a teacher or an expert.

On analysis, suggestions for remedial actions in the light of their relationship to the improvement of instruction have to be carried out to judge the sufficiency and adequacy of the tool. A good teacher could do this easily without hindering the curiosity and ability of the brilliant ones in the class. The success of a teacher depends on how well he/she performs this task.

THEMES AND CONTENT OF DIAGNOSTIC TESTING

The analysis, identification, and measurement of the abilities that underline and condition educational achievement unquestionably constitute the high point of the use of tests in educational practice. Forming the background of practically all possibilities of learning is that curiously interwoven maze of traits, tendencies, and mental abilities. Naturally enough, instruments designed to sample into this field constitute an important unit of the teacher's diagnostic equipment. Some important areas that constitute the content of diagnostic testing and remedial teaching are discussed below.

(a) *Intelligence*: The acceptance of the definition of intelligence as the capacity or power of the individual to learn or to adapt himself/herself to new situations makes it relatively easy to set up devices for its measurement and interpretation. Intelligence tests are incapable of securing a direct measure of capacity unaffected by experience and training. They measure neither the actual process of learning, nor the quality of the learning equipment directly, but they provide the basis for inferences about the equipment from the amount of learning that has taken place under certain conditions. The value of the intelligence test, carefully used and critically interpreted, constitutes an effective and useful instrument for classroom diagnosis.

(b) *Personality*: In the sense that an individual's personality is revealed in all his/her behaviour, this aspect of classroom measurement is all-inclusive. In a somewhat narrower sense, personality has to do with such forms of behaviour as attitudes, interests, and emotional adjustment, all of which are important considerations in the classroom. Personality inventories and scales afford evidence of types not realized from intelligence or achievement tests which teachers should find valuable in the guidance and adjustment of their pupils.

(c) *Achievement in Specific Subjects*: It is now possible to evaluate achievement and to diagnose disabilities with practical accuracy in the fields of whole numbers, fractions, decimals, percentage, mensuration, interest and problem-solving in Arithmetic. The subject lends itself well to analysis and identification of specific skills, and thus to diagnosis. In other subjects, such as language, a similarly exact identification of skills has not been accomplished, although some progress has been made in the analysis of factors underlying achievement in broad skill areas in it. Tests capable of furnishing results accurate for individual diagnosis are available for such reading skills as word meaning, sentence meaning, paragraph, comprehension, rate of reading, and for certain of the more mechanical elements of written language. These skills have been analyzed and can be measured with reasonable success.

(d) *General Educational Achievement:* While the emphasis is somewhat more on the measurement of the specific rather than the general aspects of school accomplishments, there is a recognizable need for the measurement of the latter. For general survey purposes, for evaluation of curricular content, and for later individual detailed diagnosis, such general achievement tests are valuable. This, of course, includes the three areas mentioned above.

REMEDIATION

The question "After testing, what?" is at the back of the

mind of every classroom teacher and every supervisor. Much of the early use of tests was futile, since such broad and vague phases of educational achievement were tested that, even though reliable results were obtained, nothing specific could be done about the situation. Furthermore, a great deal of the early use of tests in the classroom was a matter of satisfying curiosity. Teachers have a right to expect that something tangible will be given to them in return for student time spent in testing. students themselves have some rights in the matter. One way to ensure this return is for the teachers themselves to take an active part in the programme. A type of training, an attitude towards their profession, a clearer insight into the difficulties faced by their pupils, are thereby gained, which may not come to them in any other way.

The results of supervisory tests given periodically for the purpose of checking the efficiency of pupil learning should be revealed to the teacher and the students in terms of specific suggestions for the further improvement of the situation. Instructional and diagnostic tests used by teachers in the classroom should furnish such specific information concerning the abilities and limitations of their students that a programme of preventive and corrective instruction can be begun at once.

Remedial Drill

There are in general two ways of maintaining a high level of pupil achievement in any subject after direct instruction has been discontinued. These are (1) broad, general drill with no integral units of testing to discover breakdowns in pupil mastery, and (2) systematic remedial drill devices to fight forgetting, plus diagnostic testing to discover the exact causes of weaknesses when such weaknesses begin to cause poor work on review drills. The first method involves the systematic use of properly distributed general practice over the complete function. The second involves the periodic location of the specific defects of each pupil by means of diagnostic tests and the immediate correction of these defects by the use of a properly constructed remedial drill.

Unquestionably, the latter is the more economical method of maintaining mastery of desired skills on the part of pupils. It is obvious that general review is valuable at times, but just to review with no specific idea of what the review is to accomplish is too naive and hopeful to be effective.

Steps in Remediation

The programme that coincides most closely with the experience of successful teachers and with a sound psychology of learning calls for the following steps in the order indicated: (1) teach, (2) review, (3) test for weaknesses whenever they appear, and (4) follow with remedial drill units oh the specific weaknesses revealed by the tests.

It may be worth while to note that material so constructed as to be effective for remedial purposes is also sound enough to be used for initial instruction. In fact, the chief distinction between good content for initial teaching purposes and remedial drill purposes is evident when they are to be used. The most effective remedial drill for the pupil who does not have an adequate sight-meaning vocabulary for silent reading purposes is a drill on the vocabulary he/she should have learned in the first place.

Effective Remedial Material

If remedial work is to be effective, drills of established validity must be provided for each specific skill which conditions achievement in the subject. The validity of drill material depends to a large degree upon the accuracy and completeness with which the analysis of skills is made. Difficulties in subject units which can be identified in only a vague manner cannot be remedied except by chance. Drills must closely parallel the skills they are supposed to remedy. For instance, if mastery of a certain minimal vocabulary is essential to effective silent reading 'comprehension, then drill on those particular words that constitute special weakness should lake precedence over other drills.

Theoretically, perfect validity of drill material can be achieved only by taking a 100 per cent sampling of all of the possible basic facts or skills in the particular field. Naturally, it is impossible to take such a large sampling that all of the most frequently used and most important facts are included. Subject fields vary widely in the way in which they lend themselves to sampling of this kind. In fields such as Reading or Language, a complete sampling is almost impossible to obtain. On the other hand, many of the basic facts in Arithmetic are so readily identified that they may be sampled 100 per cent without difficulty.

Properly designed remedial and corrective drill material wastes no time on skills that need no practice, but strikes directly at the heart of the problem. Remedial drills in which careful control is kept over the distribution of practice on the basic skills are almost certain to be more effective than random exercise, even assuming in both cases that suitable motivation for improvement is provided. That drill will be most productive which most nearly provides a complete coverage of skills of basic importance in the hierarchy of habits upon which successful achievement in the subject depends. Poorly organized drills may or may not deal with all possible weaknesses, but they are almost certain to waste time on skills that are not in need of drill.

The validity of the drill depends upon the degree to which this sampling covers the basic or fundamental skills and the degree to which the exercises themselves actually develop the skills they proposed to develop. There are a number of places in which this complex chain may break. The task of diagnostic and remedial treatment is to locate and repair quickly those links of the chain that have snapped under stress, or have rusted out through lack of use. Correctly designed remedial material will not only parallel valid drill on the correct skill, but it will also cover all of the basic aspects of the skills. Furthermore, it should acquaint the child with the most important variants of each situation.

Effective remedial material must not only cover in a valid manner all of the basic or underlying skills upon which achievement in the field depends, bat it must provide a means for bringing about a gradual union of these component elements into the total function. It is entirely possible that a mastery of the subsidiary skills involved might result in only a partial control of the end product, if that goal were not reached by the gradual bringing together of each distinct skill in its relation to the whole process.

7

Aptitude Tests

An aptitude is an innate component of a competency to do a certain kind of work at a certain level. Aptitudes may be physical or mental. Aptitude is not knowledge, understanding, learned or acquired abilities (skills) or attitude. The innate nature of aptitude is in contrast to achievement, which represents knowledge or ability that is gained.

Aptitude and intelligence quotient are related, and in some ways opposite views of human mental ability. Whereas intelligence quotient sees intelligence as being a single measurable characteristic affecting all mental ability, aptitude refers to one of many different characteristics which can be independent of each other, such as aptitude for military flight, air traffic control, or computer programming. This is more similar to the theory of multiple intelligences.

Concerning a single measurable characteristic affecting all mental ability, causal analysis of any group of intelligence test scores will nearly always show them to be highly correlated. In the context of an aptitude test the "high" and "low" scores are usually not far apart, because all ability test scores tend to be correlated. Aptitude is better applied intra-individually to determine what tasks a given individual is more skilled at performing. Inter-individual aptitude differences are typically not very significant due to IQ differences.

WHAT IS APTITUDE ASSESSMENT?

Suppose that two persons of equal intelligence have the same opportunities to learn a job or develop a skill. They attend the same on-the-job training or classes, study the same material, and practice the same length of time. One of them acquires the knowledge or skill easily; the other has difficulty and takes more time, if they ever master the skill. These two people differ in aptitude for this type of work or skill acquisition.

Aptitude is variously defined as innate learning ability, the specific ability needed to facilitate learning a job, aptness, knack, suitability, readiness, tendency, natural or acquired disposition or capacity for a particular activity, or innate component of a competency.

Aptitude assessments are used to predict success or failure in an undertaking. For vocational/career guidance and planning they are used to measure different aptitudes such as general learning ability, numerical ability, verbal ability, spatial perception, and clerical perception. Objective aptitude tests are based on timed sub-tests—results are compared to age-group norms or other criteria—as opposed to self-report inventories of abilities often found in computerized career exploration systems. For helping a person find and pursue a career, course of study, or work experience programme; aptitude assessment should logically precede achievement testing or skills assessment.

APTITUDE TESTS AND CAREER-MAKING

We all know how important it is to hire the right person for a job. Someone who doesn't have the right skills for a position, or who isn't a good fit with the corporate culture, often ends up being replaced. Then you need to fill the position again, and turnover costs and lost opportunities can be significant.

To make better hiring decisions and avoid high job turnover rates, organizations often use ability testing. Companies also use these tests for promoting and training. The goal is to get the right people, with the right skills, in the right jobs.

Traditionally, the process for assessing current or prospective workers has been subjective. Managers use their feelings, observations, judgements, and life experiences to evaluate candidates. For example, when you interview someone, you try to be objective—but you know that your personal beliefs and values often keep you from being totally objective.

So, how can you be more 'scientific' about evaluating people? Psychological testing offers a way to go beyond the subjective—and find a more objective way to assess someone's personal attributes. Even then, subjectivity is still part of the process, but that's not always a bad thing. It would be unwise to completely ignore our perceptions and feelings about others. However, our perceptions can benefit from a little objectivity.

Interest and aptitude are not the same thing. You may be interested in auto mechanics, but if you have low manual dexterity, then you're unlikely to show much aptitude for it, so you have a low potential for success.

On the other hand, a high aptitude for a certain hobby or profession also doesn't guarantee success. A person generally has to be interested in something to be motivated to do it well.

When using aptitude tests, it's important to remember that both interest and aptitude are necessary conditions for successful performance—but neither is sufficient on its own.

Aptitude career tests measure your readiness to perform well in a given situation or a particular domain. Your ability to comprehend instructions, to apply previously acquired knowledge and skills, to make good inferences and to manage your emotions while doing any of these objects can be defined as your aptitude.

The career aptitude tests focus upon your analytical and abstract reasoning with reference to your verbal, numerical and spatial abilities. They are used to predict your future performance for leadership, mechanical, clerical, electrical and other specific fields.

Aptitude Career Tests vs. Attainment Tests

The attainment assessment includes your testimonials and testing of your academic achievements. The scales to predict the achievement in reading, mathematics, social studies and science should the same (or similar) for the people from all groups.

The aptitude career tests are means to analyze your specific or general capabilities to predict your future performance. They may differ for different groups depending upon their cultures and difference of circumstances. However, they have become an essential part of all psychological assessments.

Aptitude Career Tests vs. IQ Tests

The IQ Tests analyze your mental development to classify you as genius, average or even idiot. However, career aptitude tests do the same with intent to predict your future performance for a specific role. The former tries to express your intelligence with a numerical expression. The later calculates your score to see your comparative development of mental capabilities with other test takers.

In most of the cases the aptitude tests are the same as IQ tests. However, due to courts' rulings, they neither use word of IQ nor interpret their scores as IQ scores are believed for.

How to Encounter An Aptitude Career Test?

Before starting your aptitude session, you shall be offered a solved practice question. The tester shall help you to understand the requirements of the examination. Then you will be delivered with a long multiple choices questionnaire to answer all of the items, within a time limit. Most probably you shall be unable to answer them all.

Maximum numbers of questions are deliberately delivered to assess how well you handle a stressful situation. Besides, this strategy tests your accuracy as well as speed. You may find certain items difficult to make a correct decision.

Simply skip them and come back, if possible, by finishing the remaining part of the session. Keep in mind that it is not your speed but correct answers that help the psychologists to predict your future potentials. The aptitude career test questionnaire is built in a way that difficulty level rises from beginning to the end.

Ideally the career aptitude test results are used to analyze your reasoning capabilities on three levels. Your capabilities are compared with:

(1) The pre-set requirements for the job.

(2) The scores of the previously employed people, and

(3) The average score across the candidates.

What Characteristics Aptitude Career Tests Analyze?

The aptitude career tests try to determine how well you likely perform a role in future. They analyze your skills including your verbal, numerical and spatial capabilities. They focus upon:

- Your capability to think logically and analyze correctly.
- Your areas of strength and weaknesses.
- Your leadership qualities.
- Your comprehension and communication skills.
- Your capabilities that may be improved, and
- Your hidden potentials for your specific role.

The modern day psychology testing companies have devised specific aptitude career tests for specific jobs. You need not to take leadership aptitude tests to qualify for a clerical or mechanical post. The specialization helps the employers to make optimally best decisions within the shortest possible time.

Your mental alertness, business potential, memory, vocabulary, perception and mechanical Interests. They also measure your personality traits including your work habits, emotional balance, nervous strength, character, sociability, dominance, competitiveness, initiative, stamina, work motivation etc.

TYPES OF APTITUDE TESTS

There are many aptitude tests for many types of skills. The best way to choose a test is to first consider what you want to determine. Some common aptitude tests are discribed below:

General Aptitude Test Battery

GATB, the General Aptitude Test Battery, is used for vocational counseling, rehabilitation, and occupational selection. The resulting psychological profile is used to determine appropriate career and training paths.The Battery involves nine different general aptitude tests by involving 12 separate sub-tests. These general aptitude tests are:

- General Learning Ability
- Verbal Aptitude
- Numerical Aptitude
- Spatial Aptitude
- Form Perception
- Clerical Perception
- Motor Co-ordination
- Finger Dexterity
- Manual Dexterity

Use of General Aptitude Test Battery

Different jobs may require different capabilities to perform them perfectly. Depending upon the job requirements these general aptitude tests may either be used individually or in a composite way. When you have applied for a job where multiple or most of the traits are required then you will have to go through a complete general aptitude test battery.

The data of your performance in different areas is collected through the use of composite battery.

For selection in some particular area or for some particular occupation only a part of General Aptitude battery is administered.

General Aptitude Test Battery for Job Satisfaction

Most of the people don't attain job satisfaction for one reason or the other. However, more than 60 per cent of your time is spent on job premises. It is important to fulfil your basic desire to work at a place of your interest. Efficiency comes from doing the things that you crave to do and satisfaction comes by getting the things that you desire to use. The GATB can help you in the both areas. You can:

- Dig out your hidden potentials
- Give confidence to your interests
- Discover development needs that give you bright prospects
- Find out new employment opportunities

Suppose architectural job fascinates you. Then you need to score high in four parts of the GATB: Computation, Three-Dimensional Space, Vocabulary, and Arithmetic Reasoning.

What is Vocational Assessment?

General Aptitude Test Battery provides vocational assessment. The assessment is particularly useful when you are going to start your career or want to shift to some other profession.

General Aptitude Test battery assesses your abilities, work values, school subject preferences, and interests to help identify possible career options. It can identify your occupational interests and acquires specific information about education and training requirements. It helps the psychologists to determine which occupations best fit with your individual's abilities, interests, and personality.

Some other vocational interest tests use the Holland Codes of personality testing, which group interests into six categories:

- *Realistic* (building, repairing, working outdoors)
- *Investigate* (researching, analyzing inquiring)
- *Artistic* (creating or enjoying art, drama, music, writing)
- *Social* (helping, instructing, care giving)
- *Enterprisisng* (selling, managing, persuading)
- *Convenstional* (accounting, organizing, processing data).

Differential Aptitude Test (DAT)

The differential aptitude tests (DAT) are the latest genre of the career aptitude tests. It is realized that general aptitude tests are not such powerful to help in screening candidates for all jobs. The DAT measures one's aptitudes in the following eight different areas.

(*a*) Verbal reasoning
(*b*) Numerical Ability
(*c*) Abstract Reasoning
(*d*) Mechanical Reasoning
(*e*) Space Relations
(*f*) Spelling
(*g*) Language Usage
(*h*) Perceptual Speed and Accuracy

The Differential Aptitude Tests (DAT) battery follows the theory that different individuals have varying levels of interest and intelligence in different fields. Some may be good at math but bad in verbal reasoning. Some may architect language excellently but may be very bad in calculations.

The variety of human society in aptitudes generates a balance. However, total score of general aptitude tests can't make a true calculation of your different kinds of aptitudes. On the other hand the aptitude tests offered by the individual employers are too specific to measure one's all out potentials.

A differential aptitude test measures all kinds of aptitudes separately. No doubt the test is scored both individually and collectively but individual scores are given much bigger weight.

One can find commonalities between a general and differential aptitude test. But it is philosophy behind the latest genre which differentiates it from the others. Here if optimum description of different differential aptitude tests:

Verbal Differential Ability Scale

Verbal Reasoning Test measures one's ability to find relations amongst words. How do you view a concept? how do you manipulate abstract ideas? etc are the topics on which various verbal analogies are framed.

Numerical Differential Ability Scale

This differential aptitude test measures one's capability to interpret numerical relationships between different figures. The mathematical reasoning is also tested. one can improve his/her performance by going through basic mathematical manuals and science hand books.

Abstract Reasoning Differential Ability Scale

Abstract Reasoning (AR) measures one's reasoning when he/she solve problems in terms of size, shape, position, quantity or other geometric figures and shapes. Logical thinking is involved.

Mechanical Reasoning Differential Ability Scale

Mechanical Reasoning (MR) measures one's ability to understand mechanical principles of machines, motion and devices. It is an important test for engineering and machine operation jobs. It involves logic with motion. However, specialized knowledge is not required.

Space Relations Differential Ability Scale

Space Relations (SP) measures one's capability to analyze three dimensional figures, for instance how do you see 2D or 3D drawings? When one is looking for some job in engineering, architecture or designing he|she must expect such kind of aptitude test.

Spelling Differential Ability Scale

Spelling test measures one's capability to recognize correct or incorrect spelled common English words. This differential aptitude test is used for English and writing courses.

Language Differential Ability Scale

Language Usage Test is used to measure one's ability to detect grammatical and other language errors (using present/past tense, direct/indirect speech, capitalization etc.). This test is mainly used to screen candidates for jobs in journalism, review writing and management courses. One must have basic knowledge of grammar, punctuation, and capitalization of English language to score better in this test.

Speed and Accuracy Differential Ability Scales

Perceptual Speed and Accuracy (PS&A) measures the quickness and accuracy in performing jobs. It is impossible to succeed with office working without making and implementing right decisions quickly.

Mechanical Aptitude Test

Mechanical Aptitude Test measures your ability to comprehend simple mechanical and physical principles. It focuses upon your motivation for machines and interest in movement of their components. The scores are used to predict your future performance and learning potentials in mechanical tasks.

Usage of Mechanical Aptitude Testing

1. Screening for Mechanical Jobs

For mechanical situations, you are required not only to qualify a mechanical test but also score better than other applicants. You are screened for such jobs in army, navy, air-force, and private and public organizations. Different level of knowledge is required for different jobs such as welding, mechanical, electrical, plumbing, hydraulics, map-reading etc. However, you are analyzed for your working knowledge of mechanics instead of academic depth.

2. Mechanical Training

The application of mechanical aptitude testing is not restricted to the fresh recruitment. Sometimes, managers introduce new machines and need to train people already working with the organization. The aptitude testing sessions determine your capability to learn complex mechanical expertise. This saves employers money and time which they could have wasted otherwise on training wrong people.

3. Mechanical Education

The education has been specialized. Children express difference of aptitudes and learning capabilities early in their lives. A young man with mechanical inclinations is the best candidate for future mechanical career. Early choice of the right career can result not only in better performance but also a satisfied population.

4. Psychological Studies

Two most prominent mechanical aptitude tests; Bennett Mechanical Comprehension Test (BMCT) and Wiesen Test of Mechanical Aptitude (WTMA), are used for different psychological studies and experiments. Due to their objectivity and validity, they have become excellent tools for controlled studies and verification of different hypothesis.

Different Formats

1. Most of the mechanical tests are administered in written format with paper and pencil, or computer and mouse. You are required to identify and mark the correct logical solutions for the proposed mechanical problem.
2. Most of the mechanical aptitude questionnaires are administered to groups as well as individuals effectively. However, some of them are applied to the individuals in one-to-one fashion.
3. Many tests consist of a number of diagrams of mechanical objects. Some focus upon describing the problems in verbal format. But their range comprises of a number of mechanical areas to make them universal.
4. Some old aptitude mechanical tests are read over to the subjects. You are required to identify the right solution for the cited problems. This format is getting the least attention for objectivity issues.

Bennett Mechanical Comprehension Test

The Bennett Mechanical Comprehension Tests is used to determine your aptitude for learning mechanical skills in your applied mechanical job. It measures a complex set of abilities. Your mechanical knowledge, spatial intelligence and mechanical reasoning are tested and analyzed. This test measures three primary aspects of mechanics:

— Mechanical information.

— Spatial visualization.

— Mechanical reasoning and understanding.

For more than 60 years, this instrument has helped organizations select the best candidates for mechanical, repair, and industrial occupations. The BMCT can help identify candidates with good spatial perception and mechanical reasoning abilities, as well as with an aptitude for learning mechanical processes and tasks.

Its focus is on spatial perception and tool knowledge rather than manual dexterity, but you can combine it with the Bennett Hand-Tool Dexterity Test for an in-depth assessment of an applicant's mechanical knowledge and gross motor skills.

The BMCT is ideal for use in a wide variety of occupations:

- Automotive or Aircraft Mechanic
- Engineer
- Installation/Maintenance/Repair
- Industrial/Technical Sales
- Skilled Tradesperson (e.g., Electrician, Welder, Carpenter)
- Transportation Trades/Equipment Operator (e.g. Truck Driver)

The Bennett Mechanical Comprehension Test is administered in a number of ways. Generally, the questions are read over to you either in group or individually. However, some testers may prefer to use tape recorders to read the questions.

Score Interpretation and Reliability

When you answer the items in any mechanical aptitude test, each of your correct answer is counted to complete your personality profile. However, these raw scores are useless unless they are interpreted in the way as manual of the Bennett Mechanical Comprehension Test defines. You are required to answer all 68 multiple choice questions within the given thirty minutes.

The Bennett Mechanical Test is reported to have high level of reliability. Not only the testing industry, the psychologists but also the employers have been giving a solid weight to the results and predictions of the Bennett Mechanical Comprehension Test.

For jobs requiring multiple aptitudes, the BMCT is most effective when used in combination with other tests.

Elements of Bennett Mechanical Comprehension Test

A professional Bennett Mechanical Comprehension test contains categories of the 135 questions into 18 content areas. Each category shows the number of question that a Bennett Test may generally have

1. Acoustics—3
2. Inertia—5
3. Belt Drive—2
4. Levers—8
5. Center of Gravity—7
6. Optics—6
7. Centrifugal Force—5
8. Planes and Slopes—2
9. Electricity—6
10. Pulley Systems—10
11. Gears—10
12. Resolution of Forces—6
13. Gravity and Velocity—9
14. Shape and Volume—7
15. Heat—8
16. Structures—12
17. Hydraulics—16
18. Miscellaneous—14

Advice to Encounter Bennett Mechanical Comprehension Test

The importance of Bennett Mechanical Comprehension test for a mechanical job demands that you should know a bit of different concepts of physics. There are some daily life experiences given in physics terminology:

(1) Inertia of a body is the inability of the body to change by itself the state of rest or of uniform motion.

(2) Pushing the roller over a step requires a larger force than pulling the roller over the step.

(3) A person on frictionless surface can get away by blowing out the air from the mouth or by throwing away an object in direction opposite to the one in which he/she wants to move.

(4) The forces acting on a point are concurrent forces and they are in equilibrium if resultant force is zero.

(5) To produce extension or compression in the spring, two equal and opposite forces are to be applied on the spring. In equilibrium restoring force developed due to elasticity of the spring is equal to either force and opposite to applied force. A definite amount of work has to be done against restoring force both in compressing the spring. This work done is stored in the form of potential energy in the spring.

Practice Aptitude Tests

Aptitude tests are used in today's workplace, as well as in today's educational system for a variety of reasons. For employers, aptitude tests are used to screen potential job applicants, to determine which employees are naturally best suited for certain positions. In the public educational system, aptitude tests are used to score students, and determine how well certain educational approaches compare to others. Regardless of an actual aptitude test, practice aptitude tests come in different forms and formats. In fact, there are businesses today that depend on people wondering on how to practice an aptitude test, and that sell sample aptitude tests.

Steps to Find Related Practice Aptitude Tests

First, in order to practice an aptitude test, you have to know which aptitude test you are going to encounter. This is important, because there are literally hundreds of different psychological tests available, and they all have subtle differences. If you aren't aware of the specific measurement tool, you should at least know the type of aptitude test, whether it is a mechanical aptitude test, or a mathematical aptitude test.

- Aptitude tests that involve mechanical concepts are relatively easy to practice for. Websites which teach basic mechanical functions are helpful in your test preparation, and there are examples of the more common mechanical aptitude tests available on the Internet, such as the MAT and the BMCT.
- Aptitude tests that involve mathematical aptitude are harder to study for. Practice of aptitude tests in mathematical concepts varies depending on the specific mathematical concept, but you can easily check books out at your local library that will review basic concepts of mathematics, complete with sample tests.
- Logical aptitude tests are nearly impossible to study for. These tests will examine your spatial reasoning, which is not something that is easily studied. If you are facing a logical aptitude test, try taking sample IQ tests, as these have a large amount of logic-testing questions in them.

Most aptitude tests are less than an hour long, and you should use this to your advantage. There are many short aptitude tests available, and properly deciding on how to practice aptitude tests does not include these short, inconclusive tests. Instead, you want a sample aptitude test to be as close as possible to the actual aptitude test that you will be taking. If a psychological test averages more than 20 minutes, what good will a 10 minute test do, besides frustrate you?

Difference Between a Real and a Practice Aptitude Test

Once you have done your homework on the material to be covered on an aptitude test, how to prepare for an aptitude test does not stop there! Don't become overly confident in your sample tests. Instead, make sure that you follow through on your studying with other basic tips on test taking.

One of the biggest tips that you have probably heard before is to get a good night's sleep before taking an aptitude test, and to eat a good breakfast before the test. This is absolutely a requirement for scoring well on any test! Without proper rest, and a good breakfast, you are going to grow tired easily. Aptitude tests are designed to force you to think quickly and accurately, how are you going to do this if you are tired and hungry? Most people do not take this simple advice with aptitude tests, since most of the aptitude tests are short. However, the stress of taking an important test often will make 30 short minutes seem like an eternity! And stress is a common obstacle. Don't let stress run you—in the end. It is just a test that you are taking. If, in a worst-case scenario, you don't earn a good score on the test, it is not the end of the world! Remember an important key phrase that has helped many people with difficult tests: "This too, shall pass".

In the grand scale of things in our lives everyday, a poor score on an aptitude test will not ruin your life. Try your best, and exercise practice aptitude tests, but don't let a less than perfect score ruin your outlook. In the end, all that matters is that you gave all of your effort into scoring as well of a score as possible on your aptitude test.

Verbal Aptitude Tests

Verbal aptitude tests are designed to measure your vocabulary, verbal skills and critical reasoning capabilities. They work out your perceptions, conceptions and analytical approaches through simple words, phrases and statements.They have become a necessary part of all career aptitude tests. However, specific jobs may require specific knowledge to encounter career aptitude tests successfully.

Every word, phrase and graph has a meaning. But you understand them in the light of your observations, knowledge and culture. You are not only required to understand meanings of the statements but also to analyze them to come up with logically right decisions.

Career aptitude tests are not designed to examine your academic achievements. But you can't go through them successfully without efficient knowledge of English language. You are also required to attain some knowldge of your applied job before encountering a verbal aptitude test. It can have a number of parts, depending upon your desired job, including:

1. Spellings and Grammar

Verbal tests work out your spelling and grammar skills. You are offered certain items with errors in spellings, grammar, punctuation or even capitalization. You are required to make a correct choice from the multiple choice questionaire. The level of difficulty rises from start towards the end. You may even find some unfamiliar words. It is better not guess too much if you are not sure of your choice.

2. *Perception*

These aptitude tests are designed to measure your perception of words and statements. They also work out your skill to establish relationing between apparently unrelated words. They focus upon your style and level of perception of words, phrases and statements. Your answers depict whether you can understand simple language instructions or not.

3. *Analytical Reasoning*

The verbal aptitude tests are necessarily designed to work out your analytical reasoning with different verbal statements. Your answers depict your style of interpreting the reports, graphs and statements logically. They focus upon your capability to draw logical inferences from simple life situations. When you are going for a specific job, this portion may contain your job-related questions.

4. *Phonetic Script*

It is not an essential part of all language aptitude tests. However, when your desired job require your accurate phonetic expressions, you may face one to one interview. The testers work out whether you can differentiate between different sounds.

The verbal aptitude tests are administered to know your verbal capabilities. Different jobs may require different level of skills and understandings. You can score better than others by preparing. You need to concentrate upon your desired job and its knowledge.

You shall find most of the verbal aptitude tests specifically built for different jobs.

Numerical Aptitude Tests

An aptitude test may be comprised of math, verbal, non-verbal or any other kind of test of your knowledge and skills. The portions which measure your ability to use numbers and solve simple numerical problems are called numerical aptitude tests or math aptitude tests.

These tests may be administered separately or questions may be included in any other apptitude test. Numerical aptitude tests assess your ability to identify and apply correct numeric operators to problems to find out the correct solutions. Here you shall read about different values and types of the numbers which are generally utilized by the testing industry to set a typical math aptitude test.

Scope of Numerical Aptitude Tests

Ideally speaking, the numerical aptitude tests should measure your numerical capability and innate math reasoning with the real world issues. However, some old formats still use artificial data to measure your mathematical intelligence and numerical concepts.

Values of Numbers in Numerical Aptitude Tests

While taking numerical aptitude tests, you should always keep in mind that all the numbers are written by using digits 0, 1, 2, 3, 4, 5, 6, 7, 8, 9. Moreover, a number greater than zero is called a positive number and a number less than zero called a negative number.

The numerical aptitude tests use numbers, number sense and number relationship in a problem solving situation to measure your mathematics reasoning. There are three values of number:

1. Local Value

A local value of a number is the face value of that number. For example the local value of 4 in 3248 is 4.

2. Place Value

A place value of a number is the value of the place it occupies times its local value. For example, the place of 4 in 3248 is forty.

3. Absolute Value

The absolute value of a number is the number that remains after neglecting the sign of the given number. Absolute value of a number x is denoted by $|x|$. So,

$|x| = x$ if x is positive $|x| = -x$ if x is negative

For example

$|35| = 35$ and $|-35| = +35$

APTITUDE VS. SKILLS TESTING

An aptitude assessment test helps to objectively clarify what you would like to do and would likely succeed in. It is used to objectively plan for future learning and work. It is a career guidance test.

A skills test tells you what you can do now, given your previous learning. If you have not had much previous learning, it can only tell you that you lack skills—but not your potential or what your innate strengths are. Despite its backward focus, skills assessments are often used as a screening test for employers (incumbent scores provide a criterion reference) and a prescriptive test for educators.

For helping individuals find a job or enter training, this kind of assessment usually requires analyzing the requirements of individual local jobs to determine their requirements, testing the incumbents, assessing individual applicants to determine skills gaps, and then perhaps providing training to close those gaps.

Both kinds of assessments are useful (as are both apples and oranges, but you can eat an apple right out of the box, and make more things out of it—like apple pie and apple sauce, etc.). Assessing aptitude and interest first will help focus the job seeker, make the comparative skills testing and any subsequent training more likely to produce a trained worker who is more likely to stay on the job.

APTITUDE VS. ACHIEVEMENT TESTING

Aptitude tests are used to predict success in a career path or course of study. Achievement tests are designed to measure how much a person has already achieved or learned in academic knowledge. Achievement testing is becoming ever more important as the accountability increases to prove that students are learning. But for guidance, aptitude might be a better measure for showing potential. For instance, a student who has not learned "the basics" in primary and secondary education—for any number of reasons—can still have the "aptitude" to do well in a career and related studies—especially if they are interested—although they might have some catching up to do academically.

APTITUDE VS. IQ TESTING

Aptitudes might be thought of as separate types of intelligence, each perhaps having relative strength or weakness in an individual. This can be of high value for determining what training or career to pursue. Intelligence Quotient (IQ) is one score summarizing a person's overall intelligence based on a broad range of abilities. An IQ score will indicate that you are smart, average, or not smart, but it is not a precise tool for career guidance. Two people with the same IQ might have very different scores for their individual aptitudes. The GATB-related score for general learning ability, or "G" score, is correlated to IQ score, but is not considered to be the same. The G score, in this case, is an aptitude score based on three aptitude subtests: pattern recognition, numerical reasoning, and word meanings. A person who scores very high on pattern recognition and numerical reasoning, but low on word meanings, might have a high G score... but a career counsellor or automated career guidance system would not point them toward language-intensive occupations. A similar high IQ score, by itself, would not indicate whether a person is strong or weak in word meanings, and language-intensive occupations would seem as viable as any other.

APTITUDE VS. ATTITUDE

Although it might sound counterintuitive to some, there are indications that attitude can outweigh aptitude in determining whether skills are attained. While marketing skills assessment to the business community, many educators have heard employers say something to the equivalent of, "just give me a person with the right attitude, who will show up and stay on the job, and we'll train them." A study entitled Attitude *versus* Aptitude, by Côté and Levine, published in the *Journal of Adolescent Research,* found that motivation was a better predictor than IQ for skills acquisition. You can assess these attitudinal soft skills with tools like the Employment Inventory to find students or workers who will work hard and stay on the job longer, but it still stands to reason that you would be far better off with a student or job candidate who aligns their aptitudes, interests, and existing skills with the job goal, in addition to having good attitude.

BENEFITS OF APTITUDE TESTING

The following are some of the strengths of aptitude tests:

- *They offer efficient, objective comparisons*—The main reason companies use aptitude testing is to improve the quality of hiring and promoting. Tests are often much more efficient than interviews for determining if a person has the potential to do a job well. And when designed properly, aptitude tests can fairly and objectively compare and contrast the potential of different candidates.
- *Reputable tests are standardized*—With standardization, you know the test is both valid and reliable, so you can be assured of a fair process. And if your recruitment practices are legally challenged at some point, the tests may help prove that you provide equal opportunity employment.
- Before using any tests in your hiring and promoting process, consult an expert in labor and employment laws in your country. Make sure you meet all legal requirements for testing. Also, ask to see validation studies on a test before using it in your recruitment process.
- *They help you 'screen in' aptitudes for key competency areas*—For example, in a retail setting, customer service aptitude is crucial. Some numerical ability is also good if you want your salespeople to run the cash register. With an aptitude test, you can quickly identify the training needs of your staff and determine how successful the training will likely be. Aptitude tests help show you whether the training program will be suitable or too difficult for the applicant.
- *They're easy and cost-effective to deliver*—Many of the original 'pencil and paper' tests are now scored by

computers, making them a very efficient testing resource.

POTENTIAL PROBLEMS OF APTITUDE TESTING

— *They may have a cultural bias*—We develop our abilities and achievements through experience. And our experience includes our background, education, opportunities, and home environment. All of this can affect testing results. For instance, most aptitude tests involve reading, so if you lack experience in reading, you're at a disadvantage when taking the test. If the test is given in English, and that's your second language, you're disadvantaged.

— *Previous experience impacts performance on any given task*—For example, if you helped your mother sew when you were younger, you might show more aptitude for handling small objects than someone who lacks that experience. Or if you do crossword puzzles in your spare time, you would likely perform higher on verbal aptitude tests than someone who isn't used to working with words.

— *There's not a perfect connection between aptitude and performance*—As we mentioned earlier, having an aptitude for a certain skill doesn't guarantee that a person will perform that skill well. Many other factors affect performance, including interest, motivation, and training.

— The best way to reduce the chance of problems with aptitude tests is to use them as only one part of your overall hiring and promoting process. These tests, by themselves, cannot show a person's potential. You need a balanced approach to your recruitment and development systems.

8

Analysis and Interpretation of Test Results

This chapter is designed to cover concepts related to the process of analyzing, interpreting and using test results are outline. In the analysis process, it is pointed out that descriptive statistics are of great help for the teacher to summarize student scores in a way that is comprehensible. We have already indicated that a score itself is meaningless unless interpreted with the use of criteria. Different methods of interpreting test results are outlined in this learning activity. The unit ends with brief discussion on the different ways in which test results are used by different stakeholders in the education process.

ANALYZING TEST RESULTS

The analysis of test results enables the teacher and all users have summarized data which can be easily interpreted instead of long sheets containing student names and test scores. The first step in the data analysis is to is to describe or summarize the data using descriptive statistics. A teacher for example may be interested in only in describing the performance of the class and the achievement level of individual in relation to average class performance.

Descriptive Statistics

Descriptive statistics permits us to meaningfully describe many scores with a small number of indices by providing answers to questions such as: what was the average score on the test? Were most of the scores close to the average or were considerably spread out? And so forth. Descriptive statistics also permits us to make interpretative statements (both norm-referenced and criterion-referenced, but mainly the former) about individual scores and answer questions such as; is this particular score above the average or below it? How much higher lower? What percentage of the scores was lower than this score? And so forth. Whether locally-developed or standardized instruments are administered, descriptive statistics is important tool in interpreting the results of the results. The following are types of descriptive statistics.

Concept of Measures of Central Tendency

Measurement is the means of providing quantitative description where numbers are assigned to objects or events according to some rules. These objects or events may sometimes relate to the individuals or groups of individuals depending upon the purpose of measuring an attribute. The rules adopted become the criteria and help in providing systematic and objective mode for deriving accurate judgements about individuals or groups of individuals leading to solutions to various educational problems. The nature of rules may vary from simple to complex and we come across the lowest to highest forms of measurements. From lower to higher levels we have nominal, ordinal, interval and ratio measurement scales. The higher level scales require more restrictive rules and the obtained measurement may require one to undertake more operations.

You as a teacher might be coming across a variety of data pertaining to students' achievement or other characteristics, both of individuals or groups of individuals. We may often be interested in having a concise description of the performance of the group as a whole. In case there are more than one group one may like to compare the groups in terms of their typical performance. Such descriptions of group performances are known as measures of central tendency. Let us assume that we have got the scores of students of three sections of class IX with 40 students each in these sections. We may compute an index of the sets of scores of 40 students in each section which would represent the average performance of the three sections in a given subject." Such an index would be a measure of central tendency. It can very well be used to understand the nature of scores in each section and for making inter-group comparisons. The most commonly used measures of central tendency are Mode, Median and Mean.

If we have data on some characteristics of students and we wish to describe the group we would be trying to look for an appropriate measure of central tendency. It would be pertinent to note that selection of appropriate measure of central tendency would largely depend upon the nature of data, more specifically the scale of measurement used for representing it. Several kinds of averages may be worked out. Here we will discuss the mode, median and mean for data collected on nominal, ordinal and interval scales respectively.

The Mode

Data obtained on the nominal scale is of classificatory type and mostly qualitative. We can count the number of cases in each category and obtain the frequencies. We may then be interested in noting down the class which is most populous or popular. We frequently deal with 'scores' in measurement in-education. The score obtained by the largest number of individuals is the mode of that group of scores. For example, if in a section of 40 students of class IX the number of students obtaining the score of 55 is the highest, 55 would be called the mode of the scores for that section. Generally such values are seen to be centrally located, with other values in either direction having relatively lower frequencies. Thus the mode presents a rough estimate of the most typical or the average score in a group of values. It is not essential to have precise scores of all the individuals of the group for finding out mode.

For continuous variables mode provides a quick measure which is less precise and less dependable as compared to other measures of central tendency. If you draw a frequency polygon or a histogram, you will notice the maximum height of this point or the bar.

Sometimes the scores of a group tend to concentrate on two distinctly separate places on the scale. In such a situation the distribution is said to be bimodal and the value or score with highest frequency cannot be said to be the mode.

In a simple ungrouped set of measures, the mode is the single measure or score which occurs most frequently.

When the data have been grouped in terms of class intervals and frequencies, the point of greatest concentration of frequencies or the peak in the frequency distribution happens to be the mode. In such a situation the mode can be identified by inspection alone. The Mode is the mid-point of the class interval having the greatest frequency. Because of this estimation, it is sometime referred to as Crude mode.

Mode may be used in the following type of educational situation:

- When the most typical value is wanted as a measure of central tendency.
- When a quick and approximate measure of central tendency is required.
- When data is incomplete or the distribution is skewed, where most of the values are towards the extremes.

Limitations of Mode: Mode has the limitations associated with the scale of measurement for which it stands. Mode car) obviously not be subjected to further statistical analysis. It remains as only a rough estimate. Sometimes we may come across bimodal distributions (having two modes) and we do not easily find one composite measure.

The Median

When data have been arranged in rank order the measure of central tendency may be found by locating a point that divides the whole distribution into two equal halves. Thus median may be defined as the point on the scale of measurement below and above which lie exactly 50 per cent of the cases. Median can therefore be found for truncated (incomplete) data provided we know the total number of cases and their possible placements on the scale. It may be noted that median is defined as a point and not as a score or any particular measurement.

Median is used in the following situations:

- When incomplete distribution is given.
- When the point dividing the distribution into two equal parts is needed.
- When a distribution is markedly skewed. That is, one or more very extreme cases are there to one side of the distribution. Say, in a group of 20 students 18 of them are scoring very low marks say

15 to 40 out of 100 and two students score 95 and 100. Such distributions are known as skewed.

— When interest is limited to finding the placement of cases in the lower half or upper half of the distribution and not in finding how far they are from the central point.

Limitations of Median: Median is not dependent on all the observations and ignores their numerical values. It cannot be used as the centre of gravity of the distribution. Also, it cannot be used for inferential statistical analyses.

The Mean

Mean is calculated when the data are complete and presented on equal interval scale. It is most popularly known as the 'Arithmetic Mean'. Mean provides an accurate description of the sample and indirectly, that of the population. It is the sum of measurements* divided by their number.

$$\text{Mean} = \frac{\Sigma fX}{N}$$

Where

X = Sum of all values

f = frequency

N = Σf Total Number of cases

Mean of a distribution of scores may be defined as the point on the scale of measurement obtained by dividing the sum of all the scores by the number of scores.

Mean represents the centre of gravity of the scores. Measurements in any sample are perfectly balanced about the mean. In other words the sum of deviations of scores from mean is always zero. In computation of mean all observations are taken into consideration. This is preferred because of its high reliability and its applicability to inferential statistics. The Mean indicates the average performance of the members of the group. It is used to give an idea about how varied are the scores from the central value.

Mean is used when:

(i) Scores are nearly symmetrically distributed around a central point i.e. distributions are not markedly skewed.

(ii) We wish to know the centre of gravity of a sample.

(iii) Central tendency with greatest stability is wanted.

(iv) When other statistics (standard deviation, coefficient of correlation etc.) for inferential purposes are to be calculated.

(v) Group performances are to be compared with accuracy and precision.

Limitations of Mean: Sometimes Mean of a distribution is highly misleading especially when some of the observations are too large or too small as compared to the others. If you want to study the average class size and there are 5 classes with 100—150 students, 10 classes having 50 to 100 students and 35 classes having 30 to 50 students each. Then the Mean of 55.5 would not represent the typical case. Even within a class if 5 students' scores are 12, 15, 20, 25 and 100, the Mean of 34.4 can be misleading. There are situations where mean may not provide meaningful information.

The Combined Mean: You might have noticed in school situations that we have 3 or 4 sections of unequal size and we find mean achievement of students in a given section using the methods discussed above. In case we wish to know the school mean, the need for a method to calculate combined mean would arise. Similarly if we have the means for various schools and the district mean is required, it would also call for computing the combined mean.

Relationship between Mean, Median and Mode

In your dealings with a variety of data you may come across situations where these three measures of central tendency are very close to each other or at divergence. This largely depends upon the nature of the distribution. In a perfectly symmetrical unimodal distribution these three measures come very close to each other or even become identical. As the symmetry of the distribution varies the three measures (Mean, Median and Mode) register divergence. A very crude sort of relationship among them is shown by the equation:

$$\text{Mode} = 3 \text{ Median} - 2\text{Mean}$$

Mean, Median and Mode differ from each other on various counts. These should be used as per the nature of the data indicated, by the scale of measurement used and the purpose in hand. However, the mean is a more precise, reliable and stable measure. Its use should be avoided when data are skewed or truncated. If some decision is to be taken on the face value of data, mode is the best measure. But to have a suitable measure when data are incomplete or skewed, Median may be preferred. If further statistical analysis is to be carried out we should go for Mean. It will not be desirable to consider any one of them to be superior or inferior in all situations as it is rather contextual.

Measures of Dispersion

The measures of central tendency give one point representation of the distribution but the decision making requires more than this information. For example, let us consider the performance of the two groups of children in a mathematics test. The scores obtained by the children are as follows:

Group A: 8, 12,11, 12, 10,8,9,11,12,10, 8,10,9, 10,12,8,10,9,10,11.

Group B: 15,2,8,12,4,17,20,6,2,18,16,0,3,9,6,10,15,17,9,11.

By computing means, you will notice that the average performance of the children of both the groups is the same, which is 10.0. However, if you go through the scores obtained by the children of the two groups, you will find that in Group A, no child has less than 8 or more than 12 marks, while in Group B, there are many children getting less than 8 or more than 12 marks. Actually, the scores vary from 0 to 20 in Group B. The two groups are not comparable in terms of homogeneity. Group A is homogeneous, while Group B is quite heterogeneous. This information regarding the variability of data is not revealed by the measure of central tendency. The property which denotes the extent to which the values are dispersed about the central value is called dispersion. Dispersion is also known as spread, scatter or variability.

Measures of dispersion, provide a quantitative measure of the variability of values. Just as the measure of central tendency is a point on the scale of measurement, the measure of dispersion is also a distance along the scale of measurement. The measures of dispersion in common use are Range, Quartile Deviation, Mean Deviation and Standard Deviation.

Measures of Central Tendency can be used to describe and compare different data, but these do not give information about its variability. The variability of data reveals much more than what the measure of central tendency alone can do. The measure of dispersion provides a quantitative index of the degree of variation among a particular set of values or scores. For comparing the relative degree of variability with regard to some trait among the individuals in two or more groups, the measure of dispersion of the trait in each group is needed. The quantitative indices required for comparison purposes should be available in terms of the same unit. The measure of dispersion, especially the standard deviation, is required for many other higher level statistical analyses.

Range

Range is the simplest measure of dispersion. It denotes the difference between the greatest and the least values of the variate. As it is based on two extreme values and tells nothing about the variation of the intermediate values, it is not a reliable measure of dispersion. A single score on either extreme can affect the range to a great extent. For example, in a class, all except one individual scored between 40 and 78, and that individual scored 100 marks. If you consider the score 100, the range will be 60 and without that, the range will be 38 points only. So the actual range of 60 is deceptive. Range can fluctuate to a large extent from one sample to another, representing the same population. It is usually used as a quick measure of dispersion, which is to be supported by a more representative measure.

Quartile Deviation

Range is the interval or distance on the scale of measurement which includes 100 per cent cases. The limitations of the range are due to its dependence on the two extreme values only. There are some measures of dispersion which are independent of these two extreme values. Most common of these is the quartile deviation which is based upon the interval containing the middle 50 percent of the cases in a given distribution. Before taking up the quartile deviation, we must know the meaning of quartiles.

Quartiles: You know that median is that value of the variate which divides the total frequency of the distribution into two equal parts. Quartiles may be defined as those values of the variate which divide the total frequency into four equal parts. Quartiles are denoted by Q_1, Q_2 and Q_3. Q_2 is the same as median. The value of the variate which divides the lower half below the median, into two equal parts on the basis of frequency, is called Lower Quartile. It is denoted by Q_1. Similarly, when the upper half which is above the median, is divided on the basis of frequency into two equal parts, the value of the variate is called Upper Quartile, denoted by Q_3.

The difference between the two quartiles i.e. Q_3-Q_1, represents inter-quartile range. Half of this difference, which is semi-interquartile range is called quartile deviation. Thus quartile deviation, which is denoted by Q, is given by

Percentiles

In case of median, total frequency is divided into two equal parts; in the case of quartiles, total frequency is divided into four equal parts; similarly in case of percentiles, total frequency is divided into 100 equal parts. Percentiles are denoted by P_1, P_2, P_3,........P_{100}. Thus, percentiles may be defined as those values of the variate which divide the total frequency into 100 equal parts. So, there are 1 per cent of the cases below the point $P_{1'2}$ per cent of the cases below the point P_2 and so on. As discussed earlier, Median is represented by P and the two quartiles Q_1 and Q_3 are represented by P_{25} and P_{75} respectively. Similarly, first, second, third,.......ninth deciles are represented by P_{10}, P_{20}, P_{30},........P90 respectively.

Percentiles are more frequently used in testing and interpreting test scores. For any standardised tests, percentile norms are reported with the test, so that the obtained test results may be interpreted properly. If the percentile rank of an individual is 60, we come to know that 60 per cent of the students have scored less than that individual. If only the score of an individual is given, it is difficult to judge the performance. It can be judged only with reference to a particular group. However, with the help of the cumulative percentage curve, we can find the percentile rank of that individual and judge the performance on that basis.

Limitations of Percentiles: The mastery of an individual is not judged by the use of percentiles, as the same person in a poor group will show better rank and in an excellent group will show comparatively poorer rank. Also, as in case of simple ranks the difference in percentile ranks at different intervals are not equal.! As an example, $P_{100}-P_{90}$ is not comparable to P_{50}-P_{40}. The position of a student on total achievement cannot be calculated from percentiles given in several tests.

Mean Deviation

The distance of a score from a central point is called a deviation. The simplest way to take into consideration the variation of all the values in a distribution is to find the mean of all the deviations of these values from a selected point of central tendency. Usually, the deviation is taken from the mean of the distribution. The average of the deviations of all values from the arithmetic mean is known as mean deviation or average deviation.

The measure of central tendency is such a point on the scale of measurement on both sides of which there are a number of values. So, the deviations from this point, will be in opposite directions, both positive and negative. If the score is denoted by X, and the mean by M, then X-M denotes the deviation of scores from the mean. The deviation, where mean is greater than the score, will be negative. By definition of the mean, as measure of central tendency, the algebraic sum of all these deviations will come out to be zero, as the deviations on both the sides are equal.; To avoid this problem, the absolute values of these deviations, i.e. |X-M| irrespective of their sign is taken into consideration. Thus,

Mean Deviation =

Where X is the score, M is the mean and N is the total frequency.

Mean deviation is the simplest measure of dispersion that takes into account all the values in a given distribution. It is easily comprehensible even by a person not well versed in statistics, but it has some limitations also. First, as it takes into account the absolute values of deviations, without considering the sign of the deviation, it is unwieldy in mathematical operations. So, it is used only as a descriptive measure of variability. Second, it is influenced by extreme values. But this influence is less than the influence on some other measures of dispersion which also take into consideration all the values.

For interpreting the mean deviation, it is always better to look into it along with the mean and the number of cases. Mean is required because the mean and the mean deviation are respectively the point and the distance on the same scale of measurement. Without mean, the mean deviation cannot fee interpreted, as there is no clue for the scale of measurement or the unit of measurement. The number of cases is important because the measure of dispersion depends on it. For less number of cases, the measure is likely to be more.

Standard Deviation

Out of several measures of dispersion, the most

frequently used measure is 'standard deviation'. It is also the most important because of being the only measure of dispersion amenable to algebraic treatment. Here also, the deviations of all the values from the mean of the distribution are considered. However, the total deviation of all the values from the mean viz. Σ (X -M) is always zero. In the case of mean deviation, this problem was overcome by taking the absolute values of deviations from mean and by calculating $\Sigma|X - M|$. Another alternative to overcome this problem is to take squared deviation as the square of a number—positive or negative—is always positive. Moreover, squaring of deviation makes the measure more sensitive, as any change in value affects it to a larger extent. So in case of standard deviation instead of taking the deviations as such, squared deviations of all the values from the mean are taken. The mean square deviation is referred to as variance. If we take the positive square root of the variance, it is known as standard deviation. So, the standard deviation is also called root mean square deviation and is denoted by 'σ'. The formula for standard deviation is

$$\sigma = \sqrt{\frac{\Sigma(X-M)^2}{N}}$$

Where, X is the value of the variate, M is the mean of the distribution and N is the total number of cases in the distribution.

Let us first consider the use and limitations of Standard Deviation as a measure of dispersion. Standard Deviation is the most widely used and important measure of dispersion. It occupies a central position in statistics. Like mean deviation, it is based on all the values of the distribution. Here, the signs of deviations are not disregarded, instead they are eliminated by squaring each of the deviations. It is the master measure of variability as it is amenable to algebraic treatment and is used in correlational work and in further statistical analyses. The only limitation is that, the extreme values affect it to a large extent. For interpreting the value of the measure of dispersion we must understand that greater the value of 'σ' the more scattered are the scores from the mean.

Measures of Dispersion In Classroom Situation

In classroom situations, we are required to use statistics frequently. However, in such a situation, either the teacher avoids computing the required statistic or computes the simplest measure of central tendency and dispersion without bothering for the suitability of these measures for the given distribution. A teacher should use the statistic when required and it should be appropriate for the situation.

While reporting the progress of the child, the teacher simply reports the subject-wise marks in an examination. No other information is provided with reference to the performance of the children of the class. To avoid this situation, teacher can prepare the individual profiles of the children in terms of their percentile ranks. These profiles can be reported to their parents; they will be able to understand the position of their child in the class.

Normal Distribution/Normal Probability Curve

Concept of Normal Distribution

The normal distributions are a very important class of statistical distributions. All normal distributions are symmetric and have bell-shaped density curves with a single peak.

Carefully look at the following hypothetical frequency distribution, which a teacher has obtained after examining 150 students of class IX on a mathematics achievement test

Table 1: Frequency distribution of the Mathematics achievement test scores.

Class Intervals	*Tallies*	*Frequency*
85-89	I	1
80-84	II	2
75-79	IIII	4
70-74	HHH II	7
65-69	HHH HHH	10
60-64	HHH HHH HHH I	16
55-59	HHH HHH HHH HHH	20
50-54	HHH HHH HHH HHH HHH HHH	30
45-49	HHH HHH HHH HHH	20
40-44	HHH HHH HHH I	16
35-39	HHH HHH	10
30-34	HHH II	7
25-29	IIII	4
20-24	II	2
15-19	I	1
	Total	150

Are you able to find some special trend in the frequencies shown in the column 3 of the above table? Probably Yes ! The concentration of maximum frequency (f=30) is at the central value of distribution and frequencies gradually taper off symmetrically on both the sides of this value.

If we draw a frequency polygon with the help of the above distribution, we will have a curve as shown in the Fig. 1.

The shape of the curve in Fig. 1 is just like a 'Bell' and is symmetrical on both the sides.

If you compute the values of Mean, Median and Mode, you will find that these three are approximately the same (M = Md = MO = 52).

This 'Bell' shaped curve technically known as Normal Probability Curve or Simply Normal Curve and the corresponding frequency distribution of scores, having equal values of all three measures of central tendency, is known as Normal Distribution.

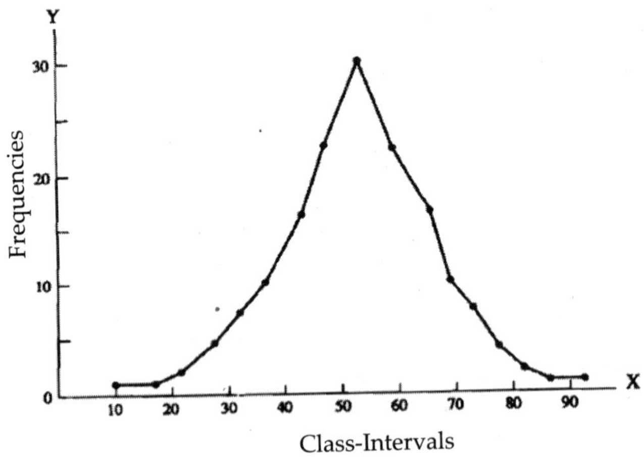

Fig 1: Frequency Polygon of the data given in Table 1

This normal curve has great significance in psychological and educational measurement. In measurement of behavioural aspects, the normal probability curve has been often used as reference curve.

Normal Probability Curve

The normal probability curve is based upon the law of probability (the games of chance) discovered by French Mathematician Abraham Demoivre (1667-1754) in the eighteenth century. He developed its mathematical equation and graphical representation also.

The properties of normal probability curve are:

1. *The Normal Curve is Symmetrical:* The Normal Probability Curve (N.P.C.) is symmetrical about the

ordinate of the central point of the curve. It implies that the size, shape and slope of the curve on one side of the curve is identical to that of the other. In other words the left and right values to the middle central point are mirror images, as shown in Figure 2 below.

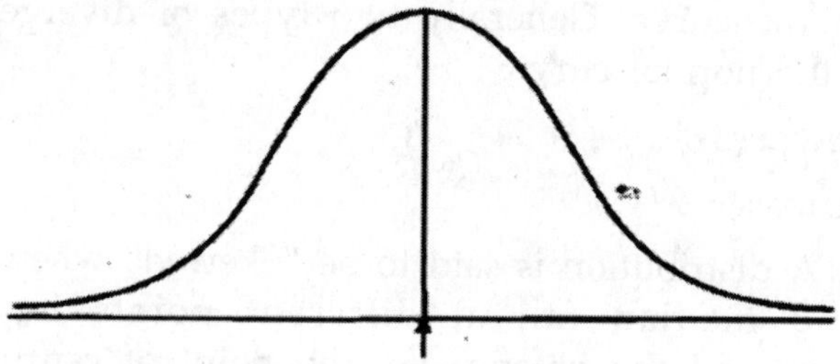

M = Md = Mo

Fig 2

2. *The Normal Curve is Unimodal*: Since there is only one point in the curve which has maximum frequency the normal probability curve is unimodal, i.e. it has only one mode.
3. *The Maximum ordinate occurs at the Centre:* The maximum height of the ordinate always occurs at the central point of the curve that is, at, the mid-point.
4. *The Normal Curve is Asymptotic to the X-axis:* The Normal Probability Curve approaches the horizontal axis asymptotically i.e.; the curve continues to decrease in height on both ends away from the middle point; but it never touches the horizontal axis.
5. *The Height of the Curve declines Symmetrically:* In the normal probability curve the height declines symmetrically in either direction from the maximum point.

Divergence in Normality

In a frequency polygon or histogram of test scores, usually the first thing that strikes one is the symmetry or lack of it in the shape of the curve. In the normal curve model, the mean, the median and the mode all coincide and there is perfect balance between the right and left values of the curve. Generally two types of divergence occur in the normal curve.

(i) Skewness

(ii) Kurtosis

Skewness: A distribution is said to be "Skewed" when the mean and median fall at different points in the distribution and the balance i.e. the point of centre of gravity is shifted to one side or the other to left or right. In a normal distribution the mean equals the median exactly and there is no skewness.

There are two types of skewness which appear in the Normal Curve.

(a) *Negative Skewness:* Distribution is said to be skewed negatively or to the left, when scores are massed at the high end of the scale, i.e. the right side of the curve, and are spread out gradually towards the low end i.e. the left side of the curve. In a negatively skewed distribution the value of median will be higher than that of the value of the mean.

(b) *Positive Skewness:* Distributions are skewed positively or to the right, when scores are massed at the low, i.e. the left end of the scale, and are spread out gradually toward the high or right end.

Kurtosis: The term Kurtosis refers to the divergence in the height of the curve, specially in the peakedness. There are two types of divergence in the peakness of the curve. There are two types of skewness which appear in the Normal Curve.

(a) *Leptokurtosis:* Suppose you have a normal curve which is made up of a steel wire. Suppose you push both the ends of the wire curve together. What would happen to the shape of the curve? Probably your answer may be that by pressing both the ends of the wire curve, the curve become more peaked i.e. its top becomes more narrow than the normal curve and scatterness in the scores or area of the curve shrink towards the center. Thus in a Leptokurtic distribution, the frequency is more peaked at the centre than in the normal distribution curve.

(b) *Platykurtosis*: Now, suppose we put a heavy pressure on the top normal curve made from the steel wire. What would be the change in the shape of the curve ? Probably the top of the curve would become more flat than that of the normal.Thus a distribution of flatter peak than of the normal distribution is known as platykurtic distribution.

Factors Causing Divergence in Normal Curve/Normal Distribution

The reasons why distributions exhibit skewness and kurtosis are numerous and often complex, but a careful analysis of the data can often throw some light on the asymmetry. Some of the common causes are:

1. *Selection of the Sample.* Selection of the subjects (individuals) can produce skewness and kurtosis in the distribution. If the sample size is small or sample is biased one, skewness is possible in the distribution of scores obtained on the basis of selected sample or group of individuals. The scores made by small and homogeneous group are likely to yield narrow and leptokurtic distribution. Scores from small and highly heterogeneous group yield platykurtic distribution.

2. *Unsuitable or Poorly Made Tests.* If the measuring tool of test is inappropriate for the group on which it has been administered, or poorly made, the asymmetry is likely to occur in the distribution of scores. If a test is too easy, scores will pile up at the high end of the scale, whereas when the test is too difficult, scores will pile up at the low end of the scale.
3. *The Trait being Measured is Non-Normal.* Skewness or Kurtosis will appear when there is a real lack of normality in the trait being measured, e.g. interests or attitudes.
4. *Errors in the Construction and Administration of Tests.* A poorly constructed test may cause asymmetry in the distribution of the scores. Similarly, while administrating the test, unclear instructions, error in timings, errors in the scoring practice and lack of motivation to complete the test may cause skewness in the distribution.

Importance of Normal Distribution

The Normal Distribution is by far the most used distribution for drawing inferences from statistical data because of the following reasons:

1. Number of evidences are accumulated to show that normal distribution provides a good fit or describe the frequencies of occurrence of many variable and facts in *(i)* biological statistics e.g. sex ratio in births in a country over a number of years, *(ii)* the anthropometrical data e.g. height, weight, *(iii)* wages and output of large numbers of workers in the same occupation under comparable conditions, *(iv)* psychological measurements e.g. intelligence, reaction time, adjustment, anxiety and *(v)* errors of observations in Physics, Chemistry and other Physical Sciences.

2. The Normal distribution is of great value in educational evaluation and educational research, when we make use of mental measurement. It may be noted that normal distribution is not an actual distribution of scores on any test of ability or academic achievement, but is instead, a mathematical model. The distribution of test scores approach the theoretical normal distribution as a limit, but the fit is rarely ideal and perfect.

Applications/Uses of Normal Curve/Normal Distribution

There are number of applications of normal curve in the field of educational measurement and evaluation. These are:

(i) to determine the percentage of cases (in a normal distribution) within given limits or scores

(ii) to determine the percentage of cases that are above or below a given score or reference point

(iii) to deterimine the limits of scores which include a given percentage of cases

(iv) to determine the percentile rank of a student in his own group

(v) to find out the percentile value of a student's percentile rank

(vi) to compare the two distributions in terms of overlapping

(vii) to determine the relative difficulty of test items, and

(viii) dividing a group into sub-groups according to certain ability and assigning the grades.

Normal curve is very helpful in educational evaluation and measurement. It provides relative positioning of the individual in a group. It can also be used as a scale of measurement in behavioural sciences.

The normal distribution is a significant tool in the hands of teacher, through which he can decide the nature of the distribution of the scores obtained on the basis of measured variable. He can judge the difficulty level of the test items in the question paper and finally he may know about his class, whether it is homogeneous to the ability measured or it is heterogeneous one.

Measures of Relationship

To illustrate what we mean by a relationship between two variables, let us use the example cited below:

Consider the scores of five students in Mathematics and Physics as under:

Students	1	2	3	4	5
Scores in Maths (X)	40	17	29	36	25
Scores in Physics (Y)	38	16	30	32	24

Here each student has values on two variables X and Y i.e. the scores in Mathematics and Physics respectively; hence the distribution is called bivariate distribution. Similarly, the distribution involving more than two variables are called multivariate distributions.

Look at the scores of 5 students in mathematics and physics. What pattern do you find in the data? You may notice that in general those students who score well in mathematics also get high scores in Physics. Those who are average in mathematics, get just average scores in physics and those who are poor in mathematics get low scores in physics. In short, in this case there is a tendency for students to score at par on both variables. Performance on the two variables is related; in other words the two variables are related, hence co-vary. If the change in one variable appears to be accompanied by a change in the other variable, the two variables are said to be co-related and this interdependence is called correlation.

Co-Efficient of Correlation

To measure the degree of association or relationship between two variables quantitatively, an index of relationship is used and is termed as coefficient of correlation.

Coefficient of correlation is a single number that tells us to what extent the two variables are related and to what extent the variations in one variable changes with the variations in the other.

The coefficient of correlation is always symbolized either by r or p (Rho). The notion 'r' is known as product moment correlation coefficient or Karl Pearson's Coefficient of Correlation. The symbol 'ρ' (Rho) is known as Rank Difference Correlation Coefficient or Spearman's Rank Correlation Coefficient.

The measurement of correlation between two variables results in a maximum value that ranges from - 1 to +1, through zero. The ±1 values denote perfect coefficient of correlation.

Types of Correlation

In a bivariate distribution, the correlation may be:

1. Positive, Negative or Zero; and
2. Linear or Curvilinear (Non-Linear)

Positive, Negative and Zero Correlation: When the increase in one variable (X) is followed by a corresponding increase in the other variable (Y); the correlation is said to be positive correlation. The positive correlations range from 0 to +1; the upper limit i.e. +1 is the perfect positive co-efficient of correlation. The perfect positive correlation specifies that, for every unit increase in one variable, there is proportional increase in the other. For example, "Heat" and "Temperature" have a perfect positive correlation.

If, on the other hand, the increase in one variable (X) results in a corresponding decrease in the other variable (Y), the correlation is said to be negative correlation. The negative correlation ranges from 0 to -1; the lower limit giving the perfect negative correlation. The perfect negative correlation indicates that for every unit increase in one variable, there is proportional unit decrease in the other.

Zero correlation means no relationship between the two variables X and Y; i.e. the change in one variable (X) is not associated with the change in the other variable (Y). For example, body weight and intelligence, shoe size and monthly salary; etc. The zero correlation is-the mid-point of the range -1 to +1.

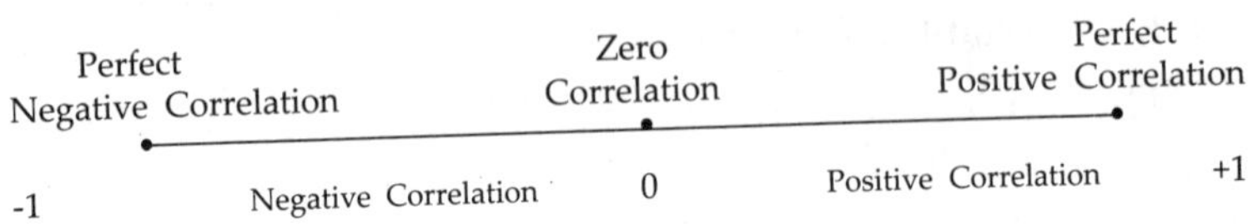

Linear and Curvilinear Correlation: Linear correlations describe straight-line relationships between two variables. Correlations can range between -1 (perfect negative) and +1 (perfect positive), with 0 indicating no straight-line relationship. Any correlation in which the rates of change of the variables is not a constant is called curvilinear correlation.

Computing Co-Efficient of Correlation

In case of ungrouped data of bivariate distribution, the following the methods are used to compute the value of co-efficient of correlation.

1. Rank Difference Co-efficient of Correlation or Spearman's Rank Order Co-efficient of Correlation.
2. Pearson's Product Moment Co-efficient of Correlation.

3. Pearson's Product Moment Co-efficient of Correlation from Scatter Diagram.

Rank Difference Co-efficient of Correlation (ρ): When the observations or measurements of the bivariate variable is based on the ordinal scale in the form of ranks, the rank difference co-efficient of correlation is computed by using the following formula.

$$\rho = 1 - \frac{6\Sigma D^2}{N(N^2-1)}$$

Where: ρ = The Spearman's Rank Co-efficient of Correlation

D = Difference between paired Ranks

N = Number of subjects or items ranked

Example: In a speech contest Prof. Malini and Prof. Shalini, judged ten pupils. Their judgements were in ranks, which are presented below. We can determine the extent to which their judgements were in agreement with Rank Difference Co-efficient of Correlation.

Table 1.

Pupil	*Prof. Malini's Ranks(R_1)*	*Prof. Shalini's Ranks (R_2)*	*Difference D = (R_2-R_1)*	D^2
A	1	1	0	0
B	3	2	-1	1
C	4	5	+1	1
D	7	9	+2	4
E	6	6	0	0
F	9	8	-1	1
G	8	10	+2	4
H	10	7	-3	9
I	2	4	+2	4
J	5	3	-2	4
N = 10			ΣD = 0	ΣD^2 = 28

$$\rho = 1 - \frac{6\Sigma D^2}{N(N^2-1)} = 1 - \frac{6\times 28}{10(10^2-1)} = 1 - \frac{168}{990} = 1 - 1.7$$

$$\therefore\ \rho = +.83$$

The value of coefficient of correlation is +.83, This shows a high degree of agreement between the two judges.

Pearson's Product—Moment Coefficient of Correlation: The most often used and most precise coefficient of correlation is known as the Pearson's Product—Moment Coefficient. It is computed when data are expressed in interval or ratio form and distribution of X and Y have a linear relationship. Here linear relationship means, if we draw aline graph by taking X variable on X-axis and Y variable on Y-axis the obtained graph should be straight line. The formula used for computing the Pearson's coefficient of correlation is:

$$r = \frac{N\Sigma XY - (\Sigma X)(\Sigma Y)}{\sqrt{\{N\Sigma X^2 - (\Sigma X)^2\}\{N\Sigma Y^2 - (\Sigma Y)^2\}}}$$

where

r = Pearson's Coefficient of Correlation

ΣX = Sum of the Scores of X Variable

ΣY = Sum of the Scores of Y Variable

ΣX^2 = Sum of the Squared X Scores

ΣY^2 = Sum of the Squared Y Scores

ΣXY = Sum of the Product of Paired X and Y Scores

N = Number of Paired Scores

Example: The scores given below were obtained on an Intelligence Test and Algebra Test by 10 students of class VIII. Let us compute Pearson's Coefficient of Correlation.

Table 4

Students	Scores on Intelligence Test	Scores on Algebra Test			
	X	Y	X^2	Y^2	XY
1	24	13	576	169	312
2	20	9	400	81	180
3	18	12	324	144	216
4	17	20	289	400	340
5	15	11	225	121	165
6	12	16	144	256	192
7	10	5	100	25	50
8	8	2	64	4	16
9	6	7	36	49	42
10	4	1	16	1	4
N=10	ΣX=134	Σ7=96	ΣX^2= 2174	ΣY^2= 1250	ΣXY=1517

$$r = \frac{10(1517)-(134)\times(96)}{\sqrt{\left\{10(2174)-(134)^2\right\}\left\{10(1250)-(96)^2\right\}}}$$

$$= \frac{2306}{\sqrt{(3784)(3284)}} = \frac{2306}{3525.5} = +0.65$$

Interpretation of the Co-Efficient of Correlation

Merely computation of correlation does not have any significance until and unless we determine how large must the coefficient be in order to be significant, and what does correlation tell us about the data? What do we mean by the obtained value of coefficient of correlation? To have an answer, generally, the coefficient of correlation is interpreted in verbal description. The rule of thumb for interpreting the size of a correlation coefficient is presented below:

Size of Correlation	Interpretation
±1	Perfect Positive/negative Correlation
± .90 to ± .99	Very High Positive/Negative Correlation
± .70 to ± .90	High Positive/Negative Correlation
+ .50 to ± .70	Moderate Positive/Negative Correlation
± .30 to ± .50	Low Positive/Negative Correlation
± .10 to ± .30	Very low Positive/Negative Correlation
± .00 to ± .10	Markedly Low and Negligible Positive Negative Correlation

Sometimes, we misinterpret the value of coefficient of correlation and establish the cause and effect relationship, i.e. one variable causing the variation in the other variable. Actually we cannot interpret in this way unless we have sound logical base. Correlation coefficient gives us, a quantitative determination of the degree of relationship between two variables X and Y, not information as to the nature of association between the two variables.

Causation implies an invariable sequence—A always leads to B, whereas correlation is simply a measure of mutual association between two variables. For example, there may be a high correlation between maladjustment and anxiety: but on the basis of high correlation we cannot say maladjustment causes anxiety. It may be possible that high anxiety is the cause of maladjustment. This shows that maladjustment and anxiety are mutually associated variables. Consider another example. There is a high correlation between aptitude in a subject at school and the achievement in the subject. At the end of the school examinations will this reflect causal relationship? It may or may not. Aptitude in the study subject definitely causes variation in the achievement of the subject, but high achievement of the student in the subject is not the result of the high aptitude only; it may be due to the other variables also.

Thus, when interpreting the size of the correlation coefficient in terms of cause and effect it is appropriate, if and only if the variables under investigation provide a logical base for such interpretation.

Factors Influencing the Size of the Correlation Coefficient

Learners should also be aware of the following factors which influence the size of the coefficient of correlation and can lead to misinterpretation:

1. The size of "*r*" is very much dependent upon the variability of measured values in the correlated sample. The greater the variability, the higher will be the correlation, everything else being equal.
2. The size of "*r*" is altered, when an investigator selects an extreme group of subjects in order to compare these groups with respect to certain behaviour, "r" obtained from the combined data of extreme groups would be larger than the "*r*" obtained from a random sample of the same group.
3. Addition or dropping the extreme cases from the group can lead to change on the size of "*r*". Addition of the extreme case may increase the size of correlation, while dropping the extreme cases will lower the value of "*r*".

Uses of Correlation in Educational Measurement and Evaluation

Correlation is one of the most widely used analytic procedures in the field of Educational Measurement and Evaluation. It not only describes the relationship of paired variables, but it is also useful in:

- prediction of one variable—the dependent variable on the basis of the other variable the independent variable.
- determining the reliability and validity of the test or the question paper.

- determining the role of various correlates to a certain ability.
- factor analysis technique for determining the factor loadings of the underlying variables in human abilities.

INTERPRETING TEST RESULTS

Three of the fundamental purposes for testing are (1) to describe each student's developmental level within a test area, (2) to identify a student's areas of relative strength and weakness in subject areas, and (3) to monitor year-to-year growth in the basic skills. To accomplish any one of these purposes, it is important to select the type of score from among those reported that will permit the proper interpretation. Scores such as percentile ranks, grade equivalents, and standard scores differ from one another in the purposes they can serve, the precision with which they describe achievement, and the kind of information they provide. A closer look at these types of scores will help differentiate the functions they can serve and the meanings they can convey.

Types of Scores

Raw Score (RS)

The number of questions a student gets right on a test is the student's raw score (assuming each question is worth one point). By itself, a raw score has little or no meaning. The meaning depends on how many questions are on the test and how hard or easy the questions are. For example, if Olouch got 10 right on both a math test and a science test, it would not be reasonable to conclude that her level of achievement in the two areas is the same. This illustrates why raw scores are usually converted to other types of scores for interpretation purposes.

Percent Correct (PC)

When the raw score is divided by the total number of questions and the result is multiplied by 100, the percent-correct score is obtained. Like raw scores, percent-correct scores have little meaning by themselves. They tell what percent of the questions a student got right on a test, but unless we know something about the overall difculty of the test, this information is not very helpful. Percent-correct scores are sometimes incorrectly interpreted as percentile ranks, which are described below. The two are quite different.

Grade Equivalent (GE)

The grade equivalent is a number that describes a student's location on an achievement continuum. The continuum is a number line that describes the lowest level of knowledge or skill on one end (lowest numbers) and the highest level of development on the other end (highest numbers). The GE is a decimal number that describes performance in terms of grade level and months. For example, if a sixth-grade student obtains a GE of 8.4 on the Vocabulary test, his score is like the one a typical student fnishing the fourth month of eighth grade would likely get on the Vocabulary test. The GE of a given raw score on any test indicates the grade level at which the typical student makes this raw score. The digits to the left of the decimal point represent the grade and those to the right represent the month within that grade.

Grade equivalents are particularly useful and convenient for measuring individual growth from one year to the next and for estimating a student's developmental status in terms of grade level. But GEs have been criticized because they are sometimes misused or are thought to be easily misinterpreted. One point of confusion involves the issue of whether the GE indicates the grade level in which a student should be placed. For example, if a fourth-grade student earns a GE of 6.2 on a fourth-grade reading test, should she be moved to the sixth grade? Obviously the student's developmental level in reading is high relative to her fourth-grade peers, but the test results supply no information about how she would handle the material normally read by students in the early months of sixth grade. Thus, the GE only estimates a student's developmental level; it does not provide a prescription for grade placement. A GE that is much higher or lower than the student's grade level is mainly a sign of exceptional performance.

In sum, all test scores, no matter which type they are or which test they are from, are subject to misinterpretation and misuse. All have limitations or weaknesses that are exaggerated through improper score use. The key is to choose the type of score that will most appropriately allow you to accomplish your purposes for testing. Grade equivalents are particularly suited to estimating a student's developmental status or year-to-year growth. They are particularly ill-suited to identifying a student's standing within a group or to diagnosing areas of relative strength and weakness.

Selected Readings

Aggarwal, J C. (2010). *Essentials of Examination System: Evaluation Tests and Measurement*. Vikas Publication House. New Delhi.

Amin, Najma (2004). *Assessment of Cognitive Development of Elementary School Children (A Psychometric Approach)*. Academic Excellence.

Anastasi A. (1982). *Psychological Testing*. (5th ed.). New York: Macmillan.

Bertrand, Arthur and Cebula, Joseph P. (1980). *Tests, Measurement and Evaluation, A Developmental Approach*, Addision-Wesley, U.S.A.

Bloom, Benjamin S., et. al., (1971). *Handbook on Formative and Summative Evaluation in Student Learning*. McGraw Hill, U.S.A.

Bingham, W. (1937). *Aptitudes and Aptitude Testing*. New York: Harper.

Cronbach, L. (1984). *Essential of Psychological Testing*. (4th ed). New York: Harper.

Dash B.N. and Dash, Nibedita. (2003). *Educational Measurement, Statistics and Guidance Services.*Dominant, New Delhi.

Deary, I. (2001). *Intelligence: A Very Short Introduction*. Oxford: Oxford University Press.

Ebel, Robert, L. (1996). *Measuring Educational Achievement*, Prentice-Hall of India, New Delhi.

Ebel, Robert, L. and Fristic, David A. (1991). *Essentials of Educational Achievement*, Prentice-Hall of India, New Delhi.

Friedenberg, L. (1995). *Psychological Testing: Design, Analysis, and Use*. Boston: Allyn & Bacon.

Garrett, H.E. (1973). *Statistics in Psychology and Education*. Vakils, Feffer and Simons Pvt. Ltd., Bombay.

Gilbert Sax. (2010). *Principles of Educational and Psychological Measurement and Evaluation*, (4 edition). Wadsworth Publishing.

Gronlund, E. (1966). *Measurement and Evaluation in Teaching*. The Macmillan Company, New York.

Ingram Cregg F. (1993). *Fundamentals of Educational Assessment,* D.Van Nostrand Company. New York.

Johnson, E., & Arnold, N. (2004). "Validating an alternate assessment". *Remedial & Special Education,* 25(5), 266-275.

Kane, M. T. (2001). "Current concerns in validity theory". *Journal of Educational Measurement,* 38 (4), 319-342.

Kenneth Hopkins. (1997). *Educational and Psychological Measurement and Evaluation.* (8 edition). Allyn & Bacon.

Kenneth W. Merrell, Ruth A. Ervin, and Gretchen Gimpel Peacock. (2006). *School Psychology for the 21st Century: Foundations and Practices,* The Guilford Press.

Khan, Mohd. Arif. (1995). *School Evaluation.* Ashish Publishing House, New Delhi.

Kline P. (2000). *The Handbook of Psychometric Testing* (2nd ed.). London, UK: Routledge

Linn, Robert L. (1989). *Educational Measurement.* Macmillan, U.S.A.

Popham, W. James. (1990). *Modern Educational Measurement. A practitioners perspective,* Prentice-Hall, USA.

Rao, Digumarti Bhaskara and Harshitha, Digumarti. (2001). *Assessing Learning Achievement.* Discovery Publishers. New Delhi.

Rao Usha, (2008). *Advanced Educational Psychology.* Himalaya Publishing New Delhi.

Remmers, H.H. Gaje, N.L. Rummel, J. Francis (1967). *A Practical Introduction to Measurement and Evaluation.* Universal Bookstall, Delhi.

Robert M. Thorndike. (2004). *Measurement and Evaluation in Psychology and Education.* Prentice Hall; 7 edition.

Sharma, Jyoti (2008). *Educational Measurement and Evaluation,* Neha Publications, New Delhi.

Singh, Pritam, (1989). *Handbook of Pupil Evaluation.* Allied Publishers, New Delhi.

Smith D. (2005). *Encyclopaedia of Educational Measurement and Evaluation* (5 Vol. set) Commonwealth, New Delhi.

Srivastava, K.S. (1989). *Comprehensive Evaluation in School,* NCERT, New Delhi, India.

Swarupa Rani T. and Priyadarsini, J.R. (2004). *Educational Measurement and Evaluation.* Discovery Publishing House, New Delhi.

INDEX

38.	Indian National Congress **(New)**	450/-
39.	Indian Polity **(Revised Edition)**	295/-
40.	New Comparative Government **(Revised Edition)**	295/-
	Advanced Study in the History of Modern India	
41.	(Volume-1: 1707-1813)	225/-
42.	(Volume-2: 1813-1920)	325/-
43.	(Volume-3: 1920-1947)	175/-
44.	Handbook of Nutrition & Dietetics	250/-
45.	Development of Education in India	195/-
46.	A Text Book of Environmental Studies	195/-
47.	Teaching of History	175/-
48.	Administrative Thinkers	195/-
49.	Research Methodology	175/-
50.	Curriculum Development	195/-
51.	Teaching of Science	175/-
52.	Teaching of Mathematics	175/-
53.	Principles of Educational & Vocational Guidance	195/-
54.	Child Psychology	175/-
55.	Abnormal Psychology	175/-
56.	Indian Education in Emerging Society	195/-
57.	Human Resource Management	175/-
58.	Higher Education and Global Challenges	175/-
59.	Teaching of Geography	175/-
60.	Teaching of Social Studies	175/-
61.	Teaching of English	175/-
62.	Education for All The Indian Saga	175/-
63.	Value Education in Global Perspective	195/-
64.	Teacher Training	175/-
65.	Public Administration	175/-
66.	Public Relations & Integrated Communications	195/-
67.	Educational Psychology	175/-
68.	Introduction to Educational Technology	175/-
69.	Textbook of Food and Nutrition	175/-

Lotus PRESS

Unit No. 220, Second Floor, 4735/22,
Prakash Deep Building, Ansari Road, Darya Ganj,
New Delhi - 110002, Ph.: 32903912, 23280047, 09811594448
E-mail: lotus_press@sify.com, www.lotuspress.co.in